Introduction

To truly laugh, you must be able to take your pain and play with it.

Charlie Chaplin, Actor

Movie Guide to Romantic Comedies: 100 Top Chick Flicks to Make You Laugh and Feel Happy Ever After is written to help guide you to romantic comedies that entertain and enrich you. The focus is on 100 movies from the early 1930s to the present that will give you a laugh, possibly a cry, and a lesson or two. It may even change how you feel – for the better. Think of this book as a reference to film comfort food that amuses and nurtures the soul.

This guide is for everyone who loves both comedy and romance and ponders the riddles of why we love, who we love and when we love. It explores:

- How to find movies that fit your mood
- How to use film to feel better
- How to use movies as emotional yardsticks
- What makes a movie timeless
- Changing gender roles in romantic relationships
- Seven stories of love and how to identify your story
- Difference between a movie lover and a movie critic
- How to find movies that fit your mood
- Why men and women like different stories
- Difference between a movie lover and a movie critic
- Impact of the music score.

Charlie Chaplin once said, "To truly laugh, you must be able to take your pain and play with it." Joy and pain are simultaneous facts of real life. The best movies, like *Parenthood* and *Terms of Endearment*, demonstrate both sides of the emotional coin. Storytelling startles people with emotion, as actor John Lithgow points out: "Drama shows and makes you feel pain.

Comedy makes you feel the pain through humor." Personally, I prefer the grease of a good laugh to appease my pain rather than just feeling the pain. As Mark Twain said, "The secret source of humor itself is not joy, but sorrow."

Drama is life with the dull parts cut out.

Alfred Hitchcock, director

As a lifelong movie buff, I must admit that my taste in movies has changed with my life stages, and has come almost full circle. As a kid, I enjoyed *Flash Gordon, Zorro,* and Warner Brothers and Disney animated movies. As my mood darkened in my teen years, so did my film choices. I preferred art films like *The Seventh Seal, 8 1/2,* and *Last Year at Marienbad.* In my 20s, I loved the revival movie theater showings of 30s and 40s Hollywood classics, and the delightful experience of contemporary women hissing at laughable, dated, dialogue like "Oh, Rick. I'll do anything you say," in *Casablanca.* I adored the thrilling sci-fi adventure experiences like *2001* and the *Star Wars* and *Indiana Jones* series. In the 70s, I was a devoted fan of independent revolutionary filmmaking, like *Easy Rider* and *Five Easy Pieces.* In the 80s, I was amused when Woody Allen revived the romantic comedy with *Annie Hall.*

In the last few decades, I find movies that offer the full range of laughs and tears to be the most enjoyable, like *Fried Green Tomatoes* and any movie made by Pixar. Now, at this stage in my life, I have returned to feel-good comedy and romance as my favorite fantasy rides and perfect mood fighters in this frantic, frenetic, fractured digital world we live in today. With age and maturity come wisdom and the ability to enjoy simple pleasures, like great film. As Dustin Hoffman said, "Having fun is the best revenge against mortality."

Personally, I'm agnostic about the movie distribution channel in this digital download age – premium cable, basic cable, Netflix, Amazon Prime, or iTunes. It's the story that counts. You will find a few "television" movies in this book. How could the Colin Firth BBC version of *Pride and Prejudice* be omitted in a romantic comedy book? Leaving out great stories may be the biggest sin of omission. Today some of the best long-form storytelling happens to be on television, like *The Wire*, *The Sopranos*, and *Mad Men*. Lifetime television channels are picking up the 1930s women's picture mantle, retelling romance and chick lit tales with B+ casting and production values. Lifetime presented several Nora Roberts' romantic thrillers, like *High Noon* and *Tribute* and funny mystery films based on the Crimes of Fashion detective series, *Killer Hair* and *Hostile Makeover*. These movies offer a 21st-century take on the ever-evolving relationships between women and men with powerful, independent, successful women who hook up with men who know how to listen, respond, and respect them.

> *The secret source of humor itself is not joy, but sorrow.*
>
> Mark Twain, author

Movie Selection Criteria

The romantic comedies selected for this book are chosen for their ability to entertain you, to enrich your understanding of intimate relationships, and to make you feel better after viewing them. The films have an emotional truth and timelessness that can release your pent-up feelings and uplift you. Check the movie list in Chapter 12 to see if your favorite romantic comedies are included. It's okay if they're not. It was difficult deciding on only 100 films. There are at least another hundred great ones to be added in a future edition. Movies are all about stimulating emotions – evoking laughter, inducing tears of joy and sorrow, and raising goose bumps of passion and fear. Here are some benefits of film viewing:

- Movies are an inexpensive, accessible tool to change your mood and help you feel better in the moment.
- Funny films that make you laugh can stimulate your immune system and elevate your sense of well-being. Sad movies that make you cry can create an emotional catharsis.
- Movies can provide inspiration and embolden you to follow your heart and fulfill your dreams.
- Films can supply a blueprint for creating happier endings in your life.

- Cinema offers a powerful mechanism for gaining a firsthand understanding of the shifting tides of emotions, without the real life risks.
- If the emotions of a story resonate with your life experience, then that's all that counts.

| Uplifted | Inspired | Happy | Thrilled |
| Scared | Frustrated | Sad | Aggressive |

> *Laughs without heartbreak and heartbreaks without laughs seems like something has been missed.*
>
> Peter Hedges, director

Movies can provide a key to unlock creativity, provide a respite from relentless small mind chatter, and move a person into a place where ingenuity can thrive. You are the only judge here – it's about how you feel before you watch a movie and how you want to feel after you view it. Hopefully, you will find new films in this guide that will help you do just that.

In a book about romantic comedy, most films are rated in the Uplifted / Inspired / Happy categories. Individual reactions to the same film may differ. For example, I found the ending of *The Piano* with Holly Hunter to be life-affirming because a mute woman finally finds her voice, but my action-movie-fan friend felt it was the most sickeningly violent movie he had seen in a long time.

Life's Changes Cross-Index System

To help you find films with stories that interest you, *Movie Guide to Romantic Comedies* provides a movie reference system that cross-indexes movies on five major areas of life stage transition following.

After-View Feeling

These emoticons tell you how you'll feel when you've finished watching the film:

- Happy
- Uplifted
- Inspired
- Thrilled
- Sad

Finding Love

Teen Years
College Years
20s
30s
40s
50s
60s
70s+
Radical Age Difference
Same Sex

Relationship

Lovers & Mates
Lovers
Married Couples
Two-Career Couples
Divorced Couples

Family
Parent/Child
Working Parents
Single Parent
Multi-Generational Family
Siblings
Elder Care

Friends & Colleagues
Friends
Colleagues & Co-Workers
Community

Professional
Teacher/Student
Boss/Employee
Leader/Follower

Love of Self
Self-Esteem
Breaking Old Patterns

Work & Prosperity

Loving Your Work
Realizing Dreams
Balancing Work & Family
Collaborating w/ Colleagues
De-structuring Workplace

Transitions

20s to 30s Passage
30s to 40s Passage
Midlife Crisis
Retiring

Relationship Transitions
Courting
Living Together/ Moving In
Marrying
Divorcing
Moving Out/ Separating
Losing Mate
Loving Anew
Becoming a Parent

Work Transitions
Landing First Job
Achieving Career Goals
Changing Careers
Losing Job
Surviving Downsizing

Overcoming Obstacles

Sexual Prejudice
Racial Prejustice
Class Prejudice
Age Prejudice
Religious Prejudice
Physical Abilities
Mental Abilities
Cultural Abilities
Loss
Entrapment
Creative Expression
War
Adventure

Combined with the after-view emoticon ratings, this indexing system helps you find movies similar to your own tastes and gives you a sense of how you will feel after watching a film.

1

New Rules for 21st Century Romance

From Mid-Century Melodrama to 21st Century "Bromance"

In the 60s, a seismic shift occurred to the relationship agreements between men and women. The Baby Boom cohort lit up, went to college, protested the Vietnam war, and enjoyed free love with seemingly no consequences. In 1961, medical science had given women the birth control pill and a choice, for the first time in history, about their reproductive rights. In 1963, Betty Friedan framed a whole new female point of view with *The Feminine Mystique*.

The foundation for the ancient sexual agreement was doomed to crumble in the emotional aftershocks of these deep changes. Traditionally, men provided food and shelter while women tended to family and home. In this bargain, men got sex, emotional support, and offspring, and women got financial security and a family. Think *How to Marry a Millionaire* (1953). But, as *Revolutionary Road* and *Mad Men* vividly show, this sexual set up was deeply dissatisfying for both men and women.

When the power of love overcomes the love of power, then we will have peace.

Jimi Hendrix, musician

Two generations later, brand new stories of romance and commitment have emerged that flip the old tales of women's powerlessness and men's repressed emotions upside down. New terms are being coined to reflect the changing time: "baby mama" and "baby daddy" instead of living-in-sin couples with children born out of wedlock; bromance, to describe male non-sexual friendships in *I Love You, Man* and sexual love in *Brokeback Mountain* instead of male buddies chumming around in bars and sporting events; stay-at-home dads who gladly do the childrearing instead of apologetic Mr. Moms.

Let's look at the progression of attitudes in film about romance and the battle of the sexes that reflect how much the roles have evolved in the past five decades.

> *The poignancy of love is the unpredictable, but inevitable eventual loss — the greater the love, the greater the loss.*
>
> David Fincher, director

When Men Leave, Women Change

The 70s were a time when women's fury erupted into talk of bra burning and equating the need for men "like a fish needs a bicycle." *An Unmarried Woman* (1978), played by Jill Clayburgh, is enraged with her husband (Michael Murphy) when he leaves her for his younger secretary. As she recovers, she is ambivalent about her new good guy suitor (Alan Bates), at the same time rejecting her remorseful husband when he wants to return, because she's outgrown him.

Women now take charge and do the best they can. *Murphy's Romance* (1985) shows a 30s single mom (Sally Fields) struggling to support her son with a Texas horse ranch with the help of an older pharmacist (James Garner), despite the reappearance of her deadbeat ex (Brian Kerwin), who wants to reunite. In *The First Wives Club* (1996), after a college friend commits suicide, three affluent 40s college friends (Diane Keaton, Bette Midler, Goldie Hawn) come together with comic vengeance to get even with their ex-husbands, who left them for younger women.

In 21st century abandonment stories, women leave and men express their feelings. In *Forgetting Sarah Marshall* (2008), the man (Jason Segel) experiences weepy emotional collapse when his girlfriend (Kristen Bell) jilts him. In *The Jane Austen Book Club,* Sylvia (Amy Brenneman) transforms herself after Carlos, her high school sweetheart husband of 20 years, walks out. When he attempts to reunite, she is able to open up to the possibility of a second chance, with love renewed.

At first, when women returned to the workplace, society approved of working, but disapproved of trying to combine it with marriage and family. Women had to "dress for success", that is, look and act like a man in sexless suits. It took a couple of decades to find a comic voice for this emerging phenomenon. The new Cinderella stories were about climbing the career ladder, not marrying the prince.

In *Working Girl* (1988), Tess (Melanie Griffiths) is trying to figure out how to resolve her "head for business with her bod for sin." Ambitiously, she transforms herself from a working class, steno pool Staten Island girl with bad hair, matching wardrobe, and even worse accent, into a polished, well groomed Manhattan financial whiz. She ends up with a man (Harrison Ford) who loves both parts of her. Carly Simon's stirring score helps boost Tess's inspiring ascent.

I'll have what she's having.

Estelle Reiner in *When Harry Met Sally*

Ten years later in 1998, the Cinderella story was rewritten as a wise, witty tale of girl power in *Ever After: A Cinderella Story* with Drew Barrymore, who treats the prince (Dougray Scott) as an equal and offers community service advice. *Bridget Jones's Diary* (2001), a modern urban update of *Pride & Prejudice,* is another variation on busting the glass career ceiling. Bridget (Renee Zellweger) finally musters the courage to quit her dead-end publishing job and her going-nowhere affair with her sleazy boss (Hugh Grant) to become a TV commentator and renew her childhood friendship with lawyer, Mark Darcy (who else, but Colin Firth).

Baby Boom (1987) overturns a woman's sacrifice of her career for a family story with a refreshing have-it-all ending. Hard-charging management consultant J. C. Wiatt (Diane Keaton) unexpectedly inherits a distant relative's baby, realizes she can't give the child up for adoption, ditches her Manhattan job for a Vermont apple farm, and starts her own baby food business. She dances around a possible relationship with the local veterinarian (Sam Shepard), while negotiating an offer to sell her business to her former consulting client. Sweet!

In the 21st century romantic stories, women can put work ambitions before love and still find the way to their heart's desire. In *Something New* (2006), an ambitious mergers and acquisitions buppie accountant (Sanaa Lathan) striving for a promotion, tries to apply her business skills to her love life, with little success. An unlikely blonde, blue-eyed landscape architect (Simon Baker) shows up with uncanny insight into her heart, though he has few qualities on her gotta-have-in-a-man list.

Now women can pursue their men in grad school, but end up amazingly successful and happy in their new profession without the man. Elle Woods (Reese Witherspoon) initially applies to Harvard Law School in *Legally Blonde* (2001) to be near her undergraduate sweetheart, who jilted her upon graduation. Turns out, Elle is very good at lawyering, despite her Beverly Hills shop-until-you-drop demeanor and outfits. You go, girl!

2

What Makes a Movie Timeless?

Timeless Movie Test: How Many Times Can You Watch a Movie and Enjoy It Every Time?

The true test of a timeless movie is how many times you can watch it again, and again, before you never want to see it again. If your answer is, "It entertains me every time," then it's a timeless movie for you. Since no one can argue with your emotional responses to a movie, that's the truth and the end of the discussion.

Any movie that you enjoy, that resonates with your life experience, that gives you goose bumps and that emotionally moves you, is a timeless four-star film for you. Forget the fun-killing critic scolds who haven't seen a movie they've really enjoyed since childhood, if then. Forget the critical hecklers, who nitpick every unimportant detail about actors' appearance, wardrobe, production design, ad nauseum, in defense of their own opinions, but never offer constructive comments on the factors that can help you decide whether you want to spend time seeing the film. Forget the one-and two-star movie ratings in the TV and cable guides. Ever wonder who writes those descriptions and assigns ratings, anyway?

Movies are the genial imagining of enormous ideas.

Joseph Campbell, mythologist

The Difference Between a Top 100 Movie and Your Top Favorite Movies

In our list-obsessed society, we have Top 5, Top 10, Top 25, Top 50 and Top 100 Lists for different types of movies. The American Film Institute (AFI) has created the Top 100 Movies in 100 years, with *Citizen Kane* listed as number one. Now, unless you're a film scholar or an obsessed Orson Wells fan, how many times in a year do you feel like watching *Citizen Kane*? Would you watch it once a week, once a month, once a season, once a year? Compare this with the number of times you have viewed your personal favorites in the past year, or have you lost count? It's the difference between the audience award winners at film festivals and the festival and critic choices.

10 Reasons to Watch Your Favorite Movies Again, and Again

Here are 10 reasons to watch your favorite movies again, and again, so you can create your own personal list of timeless movies that recapture the mood and feelings you desire in the moment.

1. **It's fun and entertaining!** Any movie that always delights you should be on your list – any genre. Pixar movies are at the top of my list for having a good time while enjoying a story well told for all ages.

2. **Have a laugh or a cry and release some pent up emotions.** In this 24/7 age of electronic chatter amplifying your own mind chatter, a movie is a great way to tune out for a few hours – with no peeking at your smart phone – and emerge feeling refreshed.

3. **Shift your mood** from being sad to happy, from being frustrated to feeling accomplished, from being unmotivated to energized, from feeling confused to feeling focused.

4. **Fantasize about fast-forwarding your life** to a less challenging

stage, without the *Star Trek* Holodeck technology, to transform the experiences you are living now. The Adam Sandler movie, *Click*, explores the comic possibilities of this reality.

Movies embolden us to follow our dreams. That is part of the service they fill in our life

Delia Ephron, screenwriter

---

5. **Listen to the music,** and glance at the pictures, like a music video. I'm partial to upbeat, inspiring scores like *Bend It Like Beckham's* rocking soul-Indian fusion score, *Bull Durham's* kicking rhythm and blues score, Carly Simon's rousing *Working Girl* anthem score, and *Dan in Real Life's* spare home-made folk music score.

6. **Retell stories that resonate with your life's experiences.** Movies can recall the childhood memory of being read bedtime stories that made you feel safe, secure, and loved.

7. **Revisit pivotal times in your life** and celebrate how far you've come. High school comedies like *10 Things I Hate About You, Can't Buy Me Love, Easy A,* and *Fast Times at Ridgemont High* evoke the mood and feelings of that time in your life as easily as your favorite high school music.

Watch reruns. They replay your memories.

Dove Chocolate Promises Saying

---

8. **Recapture a holiday spirit or life changing events,** like Christmas, weddings, divorces, graduations, births, and funerals. Christmas holiday movies are perennial favorites because the stories offer renewed hope for a better, gentler, more giving world. I'm not completely in the mood for the holiday season until I've seen the original Miracle on 34th Street with Natalie Wood and Maureen O'Hara, One Magic Christmas with Mary Steenburgen, and Holiday Inn with Bing Crosby and Rosemary Clooney.

9. **Summon the courage to let go and move on with your life.** Sometimes, you may feel like you've bought the ticket, as Hunter

Thompson said, but you're not quite ready to take the ride life is offering you. So *Courage Under Fire* and other inspirational storylines like *Dragon: The Bruce Lee Story* and *Erin Brockovich* can prepare you for your real-life ride into your next life stage.

10. **Celebrate surviving your emotional roller coaster ride,** transformed. You've laughed, you've cried, and you've learned a lesson or two along the track of the repeated, slow, ratcheted climbs to the top and the thrilling descents, until you emerge exhilarated and reborn.

3

Movies as Emotional Yardsticks

Movies as an Emotional Progress Meter

Certain movies, when viewed over the years, can provide an emotional progress meter for you. This is a good thing because emotional memories are outside of time and difficult to measure. Movies can act as the emotional yardstick that leave poignant pencil marks on your doorsill of time to gauge how you have matured and evolved.

> *Romantic comedies are a lens through which we can see how we have changed over time.*
>
> Daniel M. Kimmel, film reviewer

Emotional Power of Movies – Don't Forget the Popcorn

Your emotions are engaged by your senses and can instantly transport you back in time:

- The **smell** of baking chocolate cookies drops you back into your warm childhood kitchen.

- The **taste** of comfort food imparts a sense of fullness and safety in an insecure world.

- The **sound** of a melody from when you were in high school instantly

recalls who you were dating at the time.

- The **touch** of a cuddly fabric evokes a memory of the delicious, self-nurturing of childhood finger sucking.

- The **sight** of holiday decorations bring back a time when you still believed in Santa.

The power of movies is amplified because they induce all five senses at once, which in turn activate all five emotional intelligences. The smell of popcorn entering the theater charges your Inner Guidance. Storytelling and eating and drinking ignite your Interpersonal Intelligence. The colors, symbols, and images of cinematography turn on your Visual-Spatial Intelligence. The film score stimulates your Musical Intelligence. The touch of movie snacks initiates your Moving Intelligence. So by the end of the movie, you are emotionally more intelligent than when you started, without cramming for a test.

Two for the Road as an Emotional Yardstick

One movie that has served as a measure on my emotional maturity meter about intimate relationships is the classic Audrey Hepburn-Albert Finney film *Two for the Road*, which takes an honest look at a feisty English couple's relationship over 15 years—from idealistic college students to jaded spouses in their 30s in a bitter marriage about to break apart.

I first saw that movie in high school, so I easily identified with the actors at college age – the romance, the physical attraction, the hopes and dreams. But over the decades, as I view the film every few years, I realized that this story was a wonderful yardstick for how much I had matured and changed my perspective. Recently, when my movie group discussed it, I had new insight into how an impetuous youthful selection of a life mate without clarity about the qualities that make a good partner may lead to an angry, resentful stalemate if neither partner is willing to change. Duh! Guess I'm a slow learner, but, hey, it's cheaper than therapy.

4

Love Romantic Comedies – No Apologies

Okay, I confess I love romantic comedies. I'm proud of it and I'm not apologizing for it. I love the story arc of humor, hope, and emotional evolution needed for a feel-good ending. Love is the wonderful problem we never solve and the source of endless fascination.

Even the ultra-macho, splatter-master Quentin Tarantino admitted in a TCM interview with film critic Elvis Mitchell that his love of B movies comes from a director embracing the material and never putting himself above it. For him, the critical moment in a movie is when you start to really care about the characters in the movie. Surprisingly, he cites Douglas Sirk's *Magnificent Obsession* and Vincent Minnelli's *In the Good Old Summertime* as two of his favorite examples. Who knew?

In the world of film, romantic comedy is recognized by the American Film Institute (AFI) as one of the Top 10 movie genres. Other popular genres include: animation, fantasy, science fiction, gangster, western, sports, courtroom drama, mystery, and epic films. So, it's official. You never have to say you're sorry for loving romantic comedy again.

> *Once you've fallen in love, the only place you fall in love again is the movies.*
>
> Delia Ephron, screenwriter

The Great RomCom Recipe

Great romantic comedies require the alchemy of fusing many disparate elements. Mix a director who loves the genre with a screen couple who have great lovers chemistry. Start with a meet-cute beginning. Add scintillating dialogue. Stir in plausible ways to keep the lovers apart for most of the movie. Finish with an ending that leaves the audience feeling like the first time they fell in love. It's a tricky balance that only a handful of directors have mastered. In the golden Hollywood era of the 30s and 40s, with its Production Code censorship, George Cukor made great Katharine Hepburn stories including *Philadelphia Story, Adam's Rib*, and *Pat and Mike*. Ernst Lubistch created *The Shop Around the Corner*. Frank Capra gave us *It Happened One Night*.

Recently, some of the best romcom directors have been women. The most successful is Nancy Meyers, who has created comic romances for every life stage, such as: *Irreconcilable Differences* about an out-of-sync showbiz couple; the single, career mom balancing act in *Baby Boom*; empty-nesting in *Father of the Bride*; late-life parenthood in *Father of the Bride II*; second chance love after 50 in *Something's Gotta Give*; and, a 50s divorced couple fling in *It's Complicated*.

Another romantic comedy master is New York City director Nora Ephron, who wrote the script for *When Harry Met Sally*, and co-wrote and directed *You've Got Mail, Sleepless in Seattle*, and *Julie & Julia*. A younger woman director who holds great next generation romcom promise is Sanaa Hamri, who directed *Something New* and *Sisterhood of the Traveling Pants II*.

> *The difference between comedy and tragedy is, in comedy, the characters figure out reality in time to do something about it.*
>
> Bennett W. Goodspeed, author

Romantic comedy is a fine art of telling the boy meets girl story with wit and grace. Sometimes the story or the casting may not resonate with you, which may diminish the heart-lifting effect. *27 Dresses* has all the elements set up for a fun romp – talented cast, clever "always a bridesmaid, never the bride" premise – but somehow the magic didn't appear for me. The chemistry between the romantic leads Katherine Heigl and James Marsden did not ring true. I loved Katherine in her Izzy role on *Grey's Anatomy*. I guess I was expecting the same type of goose-bump sizzle and swoon with James Marsden in this movie that she showed with Jeffrey Dean Morgan in the TV series, but the magic never materialized for me. The best thing about this movie is the running sight gag of each of the 27 bridesmaid's dresses being more hideous and horrible than the last.

As author Bennett W. Goodspeed points out, the difference between a comedy and a tragedy is that in comedy the characters figure out reality in time to do something about it. And in romantic comedy, the couple realizes how to fall in love and be together in a fun, feel-good way. No reason to apologize for that.

Romantic comedies are perennial favorites because everyone falls in love, desires to fall in love, or has fallen in love. Once you've fallen in love, the only place you can fall in love again is the movies. The story of human mating fascinates everyone – men and women alike. The desire for a happy ending, while it may not come true in real life, does reflect everyone's deepest yearning to be in a lifelong, loving relationship. Movies embolden you to follow your dream.

CHAPTER

5

The Seven Stories of Love

Seven Basic Love Relationships

Sociologist Marsha Millman, in her book, *The Seven Stories of Love and How to Choose Your Happy Ending*, discovered that there are seven basic love relationships. She found that people repeat one of these connections throughout their lives, either with one partner or with different people, without being aware of it.

Movies create our present-day idea of love and romance.

Nora Ephron, director

Here are the seven stories of love from the female perspective. Of course, there are seven more stories told from the male point of view.

1. **First Love** – The coming-of-age tale is about escape and recapture. It's about the emotional separation from parents told in movies like *Dirty Dancing* and *Titanic*, whose huge box office grosses were fueled by teen girls' repeat theater viewings.

2. **Pygmalion** – This is the story of the older mentor and his protégé. She gains knowledge her parents cannot give. *Educating Rita* and *My Fair Lady* are different expressions of this tale.

3. **Obsessive Love** – The darker side of love is caused by trying to rid yourself of the rage you cannot express against your parents, as in *Play Misty for Me* and *Fatal Attraction*.

4. **Downstairs Woman and Upstairs Man** – This romantic saga of class is one of the cornerstones of love storytelling that continues to thrill the hearts and fantasies of every generation, with *Pride and Prejudice* and *Jane Eyre* being the best examples.

5. **Sacrifice** – The poignancy of this story line where guilt overwhelms desire continues to grip audiences today. World War II movies like *Casablanca* and *Best Years of Our Lives*, and modern mature love stories like *Bridges of Madison County* continue to hold viewers in a melodramatic clutch.

6. **Rescue** – This is the fantasy of doing what your mother could not do--save your father. Yet you believe it is you who wants to be rescued. It is the classic fairy tale story of *Beauty and the Beast*.

7. **Courage to Love** – This is the tale of overcoming postponement and avoidance in later life, evident in such stories as *When Harry Met Sally*, *Sleepless in Seattle*, *Sex and the City* and *Dan in Real Life*. It's about the journey of learning to love your self first, and then someone else.

For Each Story, Endless Variations

Each of the seven stories of love has endless variations by changing the mood, time, and place of the basic tale. Let's look at one of the most popular Downstairs Woman, Upstairs Man stories: Jane Austen's *Pride and Prejudice*, the basic template of many modern-day romantic comedies.

Love is a wonderful problem we never solve.

Andy Tennant, director

Hollywood's remake tradition freshens up the basic tale for each new generation and its shifting attitudes. This Austen satirical comedy of manners was made into a movie in the 1930s with Greer Garson and

Lawrence Olivier. It was remade as two different BBC mini-series: one in the 1980s and the other in the 1990s with Colin Firth as Mr. Darcy. In 2000, it was updated as a historically accurate telling with age-appropriate casting starring 23-year-old Keira Knightley. *Pride & Prejudice* was mashed up with the classic romantic comedy movie *The Shop Around the Corner* to create *You've Got Mail* in the 1990s. The plot was modernized in contemporary London as *Bridget Jones' Diary*, a funny take on the perplexing, less than-perfect life of a singleton in her 30s, with Colin Firth again cast in the Darcy role.

So what's your story?

6

The Difference Between a Movie Lover and a Movie Critic

Movie Lover versus a Fun Killing Critic

I'm a movie lover who wants to view a film, have fun, be entertained, and savor the lingering mood in my heart when the final credits roll. My interests lie in issues of the heart, the mysteries of the human condition, and the power of storytelling to transform how I feel in the end. You cannot argue about my feelings and emotional responses to a film—laughing, crying, and feeling good. If a movie evokes a laugh or cry from me but not the critic, then his opinion doesn't matter to me.

> *Critics are a lot like children. They are brutally honest. They just say what they think without regard to anyone's feelings. And sometimes they shit themselves.*
>
> Doug Benson, comedian

Screenwriter John Ridley notes that, "Sometimes films can simply be entertaining, like *Sullivan's Travels*, and that's enough." That's why blockbusters are critic-proof. Fans show up for a good time, not an intellectual analysis. One classic example is Roger Ebert's critique of *Flashdance* as a Thumbs Down rating because it was short on plot. He didn't understand the new (in 1983) medium of music videos played out on the

big screen to an exciting pop music dance beat. After all, Fred Astaire and Ginger Roger movies were not long on plot, but remain on my delightful-every-time-I-watch-it movie list.

Critics' Opinions Do Not Count If They're Not in the Target Audience

Critics who are not in the target audience demographic have no basis or right for giving an opinion about a movie. As Robert Englund, the Freddy Krueger actor in the *Nightmare on Elm Street* series, points out, "They send those (critic) guys who masturbate to Meryl Street to review us. You don't send those guys to review a Wes Craven movie."

Joel Schumacher, director of *Batman Forever*, adds, "Have you ever met a child that said, 'When I grow up, I want to be a critic?' Ever? Has that ever been anyone's real dream? I was once on *(The) Charlie Rose (Show)*. David Denby [the painfully intellectual New Yorker film critic] had been on the show previously and just bashed *Batman Forever*. It is, after all, a comic book. What did he expect – *A Long Day's Journey into Gotham City*?"

Craig Mazin, screenwriter of *Scary Movie 3* and *4*, says, "Film critics operate necessarily in a world of absolutism. They have to. If they accepted that all film quality is relative, then their jobs would essentially be meaningless. Roger Ebert and a seven year-old kid with Downs Syndrome both have an opinion and both are valid."

Comedian Doug Benson points out that "Critics are a lot like children. They are brutally honest. They just say what they think without regard to anyone's feelings. And sometimes they shit themselves."

The Critic's True Role Is a Guide, Not a Snark or a Heckler

A heckler critic is someone who offers no substantive comments about a movie's story, the quality of the acting or the mood set by the music or production values, but can give you a 1000 word critique on the actors' looks, hairstyle and clothing. So, what is a critic's true role? In the hilarious documentary *Heckler*, Jamie Kennedy interviews comedians, directors, actors, and critics alike to figure this out after his 2003 *Malibu's Most*

Wanted movie received an initial 4% out of 100% rating on the movie critic aggregator website, RottenTomatoes.com (RT). Today, Jamie's film has moved up to 30%, although anything under 50% is considered a bomb by Hollywood metrics. Though from Jamie's hip hop fan base's perspective, it was good enough. It made $34 million at the theatrical box office and had a DVD sequel.

Have you ever met a child who said "When I grow up, I want to be a critic?" Ever?

Joel Shumacher, director

Bill Maher points out, "What a critic is trying to do is say, 'I was there, you weren't. So I'm going to relay some information that can help you make a judgment about whether you want to see this.' It's not just '*I thought it sucked.*' " Arsenio Hall puts it another way: "What are (critics') critiques for? It's to guide us to what DVD we buy, what show we watch, what film we take our children to see. I hope that you (the critic) will be in step with us, and so many are not."

So enough with the snarky, condescending comments and heckling from people who are not even in the movie's target audience, just tell me what to expect and I'll decide whether to see it or not.

I'm not a critic who is paid to use her mind to describe movies, plot point by plot point, or worse yet, a heckler critic.

Many critic reviews are exasperating to me. Publications assign curmudgeon, often academic men to review film genres they don't get and/ or look down on, like romantic comedies, melodramas, as well as teen and children's movies. There are many missing voices and perspectives, like women, minorities, people over 50, and anyone who is NOT interested in teen-boy comic book and video game action movies that fuel the current global Hollywood business model.

As a movie guide, I'm here to offer you my movie buff's perspective, emotions, and feelings on movies that I love to watch again and again. I hope that this book will help you find movies that make you laugh and cry, and eager to view them again when you are in the mood.

CHAPTER

7

Rating Movies by How You Feel After Viewing

When Sally Met Das Boot

It all started one Saturday night about 8 p.m. when I went into a video store – back in the day when all they had were VHS tapes. I was in the mood for a light romantic comedy, something like *When Harry Met Sally*, but those shelves were bare. Instead, I walked out with the great three-hour German submarine thriller, *Das Boot*, which left me feeling jangled and wide awake at 1 AM, rather than ready for sweet dreams of romantic bliss fulfilled.

> *In front of the screen, I'm still a kid. Movie love is abiding throughout life. We are lovers who are let down all the time and go on loving.*
>
> Pauline Kael, movie critic

Fast Forwarding Through the Gore

Thriller does not begin to describe the impact that this German submarine story had on my nerves and my subconscious. You see, I'm an empath – that's a highly sensitive person (HSP) who feels everything they see and hear on the screen and has nightmares about it for days later. Extremely violent movies literally make me throw my popcorn over my

shoulder and hurl.

Sometimes, I try to watch great movies like *Gladiator* or *Rob Roy* on DVD and fast forward through the gory parts. After all, it's hard to tell a war story without violence. But some movies just don't give you a violence break, like *Glory*. Although music and/or visual beauty will calm my queasiness for certain films, like *The Last Samurai* or Kurasawa's anti-war films because I love Hans Zimmer scores and the Japanese design esthetic. Typically, empaths like me avoid movies with any of the following words in the title (in alphabetical order): apocalypse, blood, chainsaw, convict, crime, death, devil, die, evil, fear, gangster, Halloween, hell, hoodlum, horror, predator, punishment, vampire, and zombie.

Better Way to Rate a Movie

That's when I started imagining a better way to rate movies was by how you feel **after** you view them. Movies are all about emotions. Ingmar Bergman points out that "No form of art goes beyond ordinary consciousness as film does, straight to our emotions, deep into the twilight room of the soul." I prefer to evaluate movies from the heart, not the critical mind.

A loving heart is the truest wisdom.

Charles Dickens, author

There are many different ways of rating movies: stars, thumbs, men in chairs, tomatoes, see it / buy it / rent it. None of these systems addresses the emotions the movie will impart to you. *Movie Guide to Romantic Comedies* has developed a simple emoticon system that rates movies by how they make you feel after you view the film. The After-View Laugh and Cry emoticons range from Uplifted, Happy, Thrilled, and Inspired to providing a release of Sadness, Frustration, Fear, and Aggression.

Ratings from the Heart, Not the Mind

The current movie industry rating system does not provide any help for me and my fellow empaths with its puritanical attitude toward sex and its complete denial of the visual impact of violence on the viewer. In my opinion, they've got it all backward. For the inside scoop on the fundamentalist religious-political clique that provides the MPAA ratings, see the amusing documentary *This Movie Is Not Yet Rated*. Nor does the standard movie classifications by genre such as action, romance, independent (which is not a genre; it's a movie production description), and so forth, help you decide whether the movie is for you or not. The current system was developed for corporations that make and distribute movies, which is not a very viewer-friendly way of categorizing film.

If You Like That, You'll Love This... Well, Maybe

This is the time of Netflix, Amazon, and other artificial intelligence computer-selected reference systems of "if you like that movie, then you'll love this one." Well, maybe, but many times the Netflix "Movies You'll Love" selections are misguided. Just because I liked a movie with a certain actor in it, does not mean that I will like all the movies that actor has ever been in. And tell me again – how am I going to feel after I've watched the movie?

Netflix has conceded the importance of mood in rating movies by developing additional categories they call Taste Preferences that range from Campy, Emotional, Feel-Good, Heartfelt, Inspiring, Romantic, Scary, Steamy, Suspenseful, Violent, and Witty.

Through our intense, sometimes inexplicable feelings or reactions to character or plot, we can recover our own powers—for both good and evil.

Marsha Sinetar, author

Film to Fit Your Mood

Do you find yourself watching the feel-good movies in your DVR queue right away, and postponing the documentaries you "should" watch, but never quite feel like running? Somehow at the end of a long weekday, I'm most often in the mood for an escape from the everyday world, a respite, a bit of Alpha brainwave viewing that tickles my fancy and leaves me feeling refreshed. On the weekend, I don't want to break the laid-back weekend spell with a disturbing documentary. Based on the perennial popularity of comedy, I'm guessing that people like their entertainment on the lighter side. In fact, recent research by Dr. Lee Berk of Loma Linda University has shown that just the anticipation of watching a comedy can make you feel better, which is about the same result as viewing it. So don't forget to keep lots of comedy in your DVD library and your Netflix and DVR queues to fight off those gloomy mood days.

CHAPTER

8

Why Men Like Action and Women Like Romance

Both men and women engage in a lifelong quest for wholeness. Each person explores this journey by shifting their focus between their inner female and inner male, regardless of sexual orientation. But men and women experience the trip differently, even if they travel on the same road. In her book, *How to Write a Movie in 21 Days*, Vicki King points out that men and women characters learn their lessons differently. "His test tends to pit him against his own life's circumstances. Her test tends to pit her sense of herself against her relationships."

Escapism has a place in movies as long as girls like stories about love affairs that work out and boys like stories about cars that crack up.

Lisa Schwarzbaum, film reviewer

Many men choose to learn their lessons through action-oriented life challenges, in which they decide if they pass. Films like *Die Hard*, *Cliffhanger* or *300* engage male fantasies about overcoming physical jeopardy. Men can compare their own life trials to those of the movie hero. Women, on the other hand, select lessons that experiment with their relationships, like *9 to 5* or *First Wives' Club*. They place themselves in jeopardy with their parents, their lovers, their children, or their coworkers. Women seek totality through the successful resolution of cooperative efforts.

The different life learning strategies of men and women are most pronounced in their 30s and 40s. This truth has fueled romantic comedy stories for generations, exemplified by screen couples such as Clark Gable and Claudette Colbert, Katharine Hepburn and Spencer Tracy, Rock Hudson and Doris Day, Warren Beatty and Julie Christie, up to present day where we are still searching for couples who conjures up that type of powerful screen chemistry over many movies.

Power of Gender-Bending

Creating characters who play against society's sexual expectations and stereotypes is a powerful storytelling device. Film director Howard Hawks turned the gender-bending approach into memorable films such as *His Girl Friday* and *I Was a Male War Bride*. Real life is more complex. One person's dream can be another's nightmare. The documentary *Paris Is Burning* shows a gay black man in Harlem whose dream is to be supported by a rich man. The Victorian heroine in *The Ballad of Little Jo*, who must pose as a man in the West to achieve her independence from her wealthy Eastern family, holds the exact opposite viewpoint in a strict society that does not allow women to own property or even buy men's clothing.

When Harry Met Sally is about the fact that men and women see everything differently.

Nora Ephron, screenwriter

This could explain one of the reasons why men like action and women like romance. An amusing scene in *Sleepless in Seattle* shows how men and women have completely different emotional responses to two types of film stories: courage under fire and second chance love. The two men in the scene, Tom Hanks and Victor Garber, get choked up talking about the final scene in *The Dirty Dozen* and how it always makes them weep. The woman in the scene, played by Rita Wilson as Tom's sister, stares at the men in slack-jawed disbelief. But she tears up when she reminisces about how the ending scene in *An Affair to Remember* always makes her cry. As she sobs, Hanks' movie son asks the men, "Is she all right?" The men assure him she's fine with perplexed looks on their faces. Very funny, and unfortunately, very true.

CHAPTER

9

Why Feel Guilty About Feeling Good?

Movies may be more effective than antidepressants in elevating your mood. After all, TV pharmaceutical ads admit that two-thirds of their users may still be depressed after use. I experienced this movie feel-good effect firsthand with *Sister Act*. I was having one of those days where nothing seemed to be going right. Living in a small town with a one-screen movie theater a few blocks away, I finally gave up in exasperation and decided to see a movie I had never heard of before. Two hours later, my mood was completely transformed from the depths of frustration to an amazing sense of feeling great. This was due to wonderful performances by Whoopi Goldberg and Maggie Smith. The delightful comic vision script tells a tale about a Reno nightclub singer hiding from the mob in a San Francisco Catholic convent. The fugitive singer teaches the sisters a thing or two about soul, set to the beat of an exciting Motown score.

Having fun is the best revenge against mortality.

Dustin Hoffman, actor

What happened? There are proven scientific studies about the benefits of laughter and the many ways it helps to heal and change your mood. Laughter combats fear. It comforts. It relaxes. It reduces pain. It boosts the

immune system. It reduces stress. It's contagious and spreads happiness. It cultivates optimism. It facilitates communication. As Victor Hugo said, "Laughter is the sun that drives winter from the human face." Even the Judeo-Christian Bible in Proverbs 17:22 says "A happy heart is good medicine."

The bottom line is, in the darkness of the theater or in the comfort of your home, you can go down an emotional rabbit hole, leave your troubles safely stored there, and emerge in a better mood. You had fun and feel better! So tell me again: What's so bad about feeling good?

10

How to Graze for Movie Comfort Food

Grazing for Movie Comfort Food to Amuse and Nurture the Soul

Selecting a film to watch in times of personal confusion and stress is like grazing for movie comfort food that can amuse and nurture the soul. Think of movies as pastures of moods, times, and places you can pick to alter your mood in the moment. You can forage around for the right match and chew on the movie character's emotional highs and lows. It is often easier to understand how to resolve a movie character's dilemma than your own real life situation. Best of all, the viewing experience has the potential to transform your feelings in a couple of hours.

Film goes straight to our emotions, deep into the twilight room of the soul, beyond ordinary consciousness.

Ingmar Bergman, director

You can feel happy *When Harry Met Sally* or feel sad in a good way after *The Joy Luck Club*. You can be inspired by *Dragon: The Bruce Lee Story* to never give up your dreams or you can laugh about workplace frustrations with *Office Space* or commiserate with the employee breakdown in *Falling Down*. You can feel uplifted by a courageous 12-year-old Maori girl's quest

to take over leadership of her tribe in *Whale Rider* or be scared by *The Haunting*. You can be intrigued by the mystery of *Zodiac*. Or release pent-up aggression in *300*.

No matter where you are on your journey through life, movies can serve as emotional rest stops from the uncertainty of inevitable change, recharging stations to reinvigorate you on your lifelong quest to feel loved, safe, and whole. Ask yourself how you are feeling right now. How would you like to feel after watching a movie?

You can begin your comfort food movie search with the passion and pleasure of films about food that tantalizes your palate, opens your heart, and makes your imagination growl in anticipation of being fulfilled. Here are 12 movies about the human condition to ruminate on and quench your appetite for comfort, while amusing and nurturing your soul. Let's look at three areas: Feel-Good Chocolate, Cooking Like the Pros, and Hope of Healing the Future.

Feel-Good Chocolate

When in doubt, start with the reliable mood-elevating magic of chocolate.

• **Free Spirit Threat**: In *Chocolat* (2000), a mysterious chocolatier (Juliet Binoche) comes to a small French town and opens a shop across from the church. The shop first threatens and then enchants the village with her exquisite confections.

• **Healing the Jilt**: A woman, jilted by her sister's soon-to-be husband, learns how to pour all her thwarted passion into cooking and transform her emotions in this sensuous Golden Globe winner *Like Water for Chocolate*.

Cooking Like the Pros

The joy and challenge of professional chefs raise the bar on food preparation as a daily practice, seeking perfection in recipes from ever-varying ingredients. Here are five films that explore innovative solutions to the day-by-day test of enlivening life's taste buds.

- **Overcoming Career Frustration**: *Julie & Julia* compares the trials and tribulations of two foodies. It takes Julia Child (Meryl Streep) almost a decade to get her *Mastering the Art of French Cooking* cookbook published, with the loving support of her soul mate husband, Paul (Stanley Tucci). A 30-year-old aspiring writer and Ivy League graduate dead-ended in a grim cubicle job, Julie Powell (Amy Smart) decides to blog about preparing all 524 recipes in Julia Child's cookbook in 365 days, with the support of her understanding husband, while they live above a pizza parlor in Queens.

> *Storytelling startles people with emotion. Drama shows and makes you feel the pain. Comedy makes you feel the pain through humor.*
>
> John Lithgow, actor

- **Opening Your Heart**: The enchanting award-winning German film *Mostly Martha* stars Martine Gedreck (*The Lives of Others*) as an uptight perfectionist chef whose life is up-ended when her sister is killed in a car crash. Martha must care for her difficult, grieving young niece. A big-hearted, enjoy-the-moment Italian sous chef (Sergio Castellitto) is hired to cover for Martha while she adjusts to her new circumstances, but she feels threatened by him and the impact his infectious joy has on the kitchen staff, including her.

- **Last Ditch Effort**: In the *Big Night*, two Italian immigrant brothers (Stanley Tucci and Tony Shalhoub) run a failing neighborhood restaurant in the 1950s in this delightful family comedy. They decide to go for broke before they file for bankruptcy and throw a feast for Louis Prima, a popular trumpeter.

- **Resolving the Generation Clash**: In *Eat Drink Man Woman*, directed by Ang Lee, a Taiwanese widowed master chef with three adult daughters spar over the clash between Chinese tradition and modernity at their weekly Sunday dinners. Be sure to have your favorite Chinese takeout menu handy for a quick call after this movie. The same story was remade as *Tortilla Soup* about a Mexican-American family who run a restaurant, with Hector Elizondo as the father-chef.

- **Dare to Dream Big**: Only Pixar's co-writer-directors Brad Bird and

Jan Pinkava can wash away the "eewu" factor from the brilliant *Ratatouille* about Remy (voiced by Patton Oswalt), a rat who aspires to become a French master chef, the restaurant's garbage boy turned so-so sous-chef Linguini (Lou Romano), who provides human cover for Remy, and the aged cynical food critic Anton Ego (Peter O'Toole), who is transported by Remy's French vegetable dish ratatouille back to his childhood. A delight for all ages, this animated film encourages adults to follow their dreams and inspires kids to love their vegetables.

Stories heal. Our favorite movies are emblematic of ideas we need to value for this enrichment to happen.

Marsha Sinetar, author

Reconciling the Past to Heal the Future

Here are five cinematic stories about large dinners, banquets and feasts that gather family and friends to resolve the past in hopes of healing the future.

• **Little Time to Live**: In the life-affirming romantic comedy *Last Holiday*, department store cookware clerk Georgia (Queen Latifah), with a scrapbook of dreams of owning a restaurant and a romance with fellow clerk Sean (LL Cool J), is told she has a terminal illness with a few weeks left to live. She cashes in the savings bonds she inherited from her departed mother and blows it on a luxurious European hotel trip to experience every dish of every meal prepared by their world-renown chef (Gerard Depardieu) and tempts fate with the thrills of extreme winter sports.

• **Hope for the Future**: *Pieces of April* shows the first Thanksgiving dinner that Katie Holmes cooks in her tiny NYC apartment with a temperamental oven. She invites her estranged suburban family and dying mother (Patricia Clarkson) to meet her boyfriend (Derek Luke) and to address her family's dysfunctional past, in hopes of healing their future.

• **Dread the Family Gathering**: *Home for the Holidays*, directed by Jodie Foster, is a film for anyone who dreads facing the undeniable truth about where you are in your life now, versus where you thought you'd be, that is triggered by family gatherings. The movie takes a look at the goofy antics of Thanksgiving family dysfunction through the eyes of the 40-year-old divorced sister (Holly Hunter), who has just lost her job and control of her daughter, and her gay brother (Robert Downey), who decides to come out.

• **Feast of Gratitude**: *Babette's Feast* tells the 19th century tale of a French refugee, Babette, who begs two Danish sisters in a small Protestant town to take her in as their maid. Years later, on the 100th anniversary of the women's pastor father's birth, Babette prepares an elaborate dinner in his honor and invites a guest with a secret.

• **Can't Come Out**: In *The Wedding Banquet*, the gay son of a wealthy Chinese family moves to the US to be with his American lover, but doesn't have the courage to tell the truth to his parents. He proceeds to marry a woman to keep his cover, with surprising results.

Here's to finding comfort food movies that whet your appetite, tickle your fancy, and leave your soul feeling nourished in the end. Bon appetit!

CHAPTER

11

Don't Forget the Music

Have you ever wondered why the movie music credits are always at the bitter end of the credits, after craft services, accountants, and other non-creative contributors? If "Music is direct access to the soul," as Laurence Fishburne has pointed out, and "an actor's job is to help people feel emotions that normally might be difficult to do on their own," then shouldn't the music credits be listed just after the actors? As one who always sits through all the movie credits, just to see who wrote and performed the music, I vote for moving the music credits to their rightful place in the emotional contribution hierarchy of the film – way up near the top of the credit roll.

Music is direct access to the soul.

Laurence Fishburne, actor

Great directors understand the intertwining emotional contribution of music to a film's viewing. Many use music in various ways during the film development process. Some use a rough score in rehearsals or on set to put the actors in the movie's mood. Many times, the movie music becomes another character in the story, reinforcing the emotional highs and lows of the story arc. You cannot remember *The Godfather* movies without recalling the poignant theme or *The Graduate* without Simon and Garfunkel's Mrs. Robinson. And who can forget the thumping music before the shark's appearance, whether visual or imagined, in *Jaws*?

The great movie scores set the mood, move the action to the next scene, and emotionally set you up and guide you along to the next part of the story. The timelessness of a movie is interdependent on the quality of the score and how well it holds up over time, like classic music of any genre. From the minute *A Knight's Tale* begins its medieval jousting tournament to the chant of Queen's *We Will Rock You*, you're ready to hop onto a fun ride of an irreverent movie about youth, identity, and freedom, just like Rock & Roll.

On the downside, some movies overproduce the music score and/or cop out with well-known songs to fill in emotions that are missing from the script. Some producers cheap out on the music and miss an opportunity to elevate a great film story to a terrific cinematic experience, like the John Candy comedy about the Jamaican Winter Olympics bob sled team in *Cool Runnings*, filmed without any great reggae groups like Bob Marley, Jimmy Cliff, or Third World. Some scores are immediately dated to their period, like the 80s synthesizer score of *Hoosiers*, that today distracts me like fingernails on a blackboard from the inspiring underdog sports story.

> *Music is the shorthand of emotion. Emotions, which let themselves be described in words with such difficulty, are directly conveyed in music, and in its power and significance.*
>
> Leo Tolstoy, author

Here are my top five romantic comedy scores that sustain and reverberate the touching, affecting, and exciting moment of the films.

1. ***Bull Durham*** has a classic R&B score that punctuates the amusing dialogue and kicks up the baseball action with exclamation points of guitar twangs, drum kicks, and sexy lyric swoons. "Oh, my!" as Susan Sarandon's character, Annie, would say.

2. ***Dan in Real Life***, with its sweet, bouncy "homemade" folk guitar score and ironic lyrics becomes a character that captures the sad, vulnerable, and ultimately hopeful mood of widower Dan (Steve Carell) as he juggles single fatherhood, a newspaper parenting advice column,

and the unintended pursuit of his brother's new girlfriend, amidst a large, loving, active family weekend in a lovely old shingled beach house on a Rhode Island bay. Heartwarming and sweet!

3. ***Bend It Like Beckham*** with its driving fusion of R&B and Indian pop music perfectly mirrors Jasminda's (Parminder Nadra) dilemma as a first generation London Anglo-Indian, straddling her orthodox Sikh parents' desire for her to succeed as a lawyer with her own ambition to play college soccer and win the heart of her Irish coach.

4. ***Something New*** offers a splendid, spare piano, guitar, and synthesizer original score. It's fused with R&B neo-soul classics that take an ambitious LA cotillion accountant buppie (Sanaa Lathan) on her amusing arc of falling in love with her blond, blue-eyed landscape architect (Simon Baker).

5. ***Cousins***, a delicious Americanized adaptation of the French film *Cousin, Cousine*, stirs up a Rachmaninoff-like piano and plush strings score with sad and wistful trumpet solos to set the mood for a complicated romance. The revenge plot shows how two unhappily married people (Ted Danson, Isabella Rossellini), cousins by marriage, get even with her husband and his wife, who are having a sexual fling. But they end up falling in love to the dismay of their spouses and relatives. This all happens between three big Polish weddings, with awful wedding cover band music, and a funeral in Seattle.

12

100 Romantic Comedies Summary

Laugh & Cry Rating System

This chapter gives you a list of 100 romantic comedies. Each movie is rated with its after-view feelings and the life changes addressed by each film.

Movie Guide to Romantic Comedies

After-View Feeling

These emoticons tell you how you'll feel when you've finished watching the film:

Happy

Uplifted

Inspired

Thrilled

Sad

Finding Love

Teen Years
College Years
20s
30s
40s
50s
60s
70s+
Radical Age Difference
Same Sex

Relationship

Lovers & Mates
Lovers
Married Couples
Two-Career Couples
Divorced Couples

Family
Parent/Child
Working Parents
Single Parent
Multi-Generational Family
Siblings
Elder Care

Friends & Colleagues
Friends
Colleagues & Co-Workers
Community

Professional
Teacher/Student
Boss/Employee
Leader/Follower

Love of Self
Self-Esteem
Breaking Old Patterns

Work & Prosperity

Loving Your Work
Realizing Dreams
Balancing Work & Family
Collaborating w/ Colleagues
De-structuring Workplace

Transitions

20s to 30s Passage
30s to 40s Passage
Midlife Crisis
Retiring

Relationship Transitions
Courting
Living Together/ Moving In
Marrying
Divorcing
Moving Out/ Separating
Losing Mate
Loving Anew
Becoming a Parent

Work Transitions
Landing First Job
Achieving Career Goals
Changing Careers
Losing Job
Surviving Downsizing

Overcoming Obstacles

Sexual Prejudice
Racial Prejudice
Class Prejudice
Age Prejudice
Religious Prejudice
Physical Abilities
Mental Abilities
Cultural Abilities
Loss
Entrapment
Creative Expression
War
Adventure

How to Use the Life's Changes Cross-Index

Movies are listed alphabetically by title. Once you find the movie you want, note the after-view feelings icon, and which life changes are addressed in the movie.

Life Changes •

Release date and run time in minutes •

Title A plot description can be found in Chapter 13. •

After-View Feeling These icons tell you how you'll feel when you've finished watching the film (see key). •

Movie Title	Date/Run Time	Finding Love	Relationships	Work & Prosperity	Transitions	Overcoming Obstacles	After-View Feeling
While You Were Sleeping	1995/103	30s	Lovers		Courting		☺
You've Got Mail	1998/119	30s	Lovers	Realizing Dreams, De-structuring Workplace	Losing Job, Courting	Class Prejudice	☺

Movie Guide to Romantic Comedies

After-View Feeling	Movie Title	Date/Run Time	Finding Love	Relationships	Work & Prosperity	Transitions	Overcoming Obstacles
Happy	10 Things I Hate About You	1999/97	Teens	Lovers		Courting	
Uplifted	About a Boy	2002/101	30s	Lovers, Single Parent, Parent/Child			Loss
Inspired	American Splendor	2003/101	50s	Married Couples	Realizing Dreams	Marrying	Creative Expression
Sad, Happy	Affair To Remember, An	1957/119	30s	Lovers			
Happy, Sad	Annie Hall	1977/95	30s	Lovers			
Happy	Awful Truth, The	1937/91	30s	Married Couples		Divorcing	
Inspired, Sad, Happy	Barcelona	1994/102	20s	Lovers	Realizing Dreams	Courting	Cultural Abilities
Sad, Happy	Beautiful Girls	1996/110	30s	Lovers, Friends		20s to 30s Passage	Entrapment

After-View Feeling Key: Happy   Uplifted   Inspired   Thrilled   Sad

After-View Feeling	Movie Title	Date/Run Time	Finding Love	Relationships	Work & Prosperity	Transitions	Overcoming Obstacles
(film icons)	Bend It Like Beckham	2003/112	Teens	Lovers / Parent/Child	Realizing Dreams		Racial Prejudice
(film icons)	Benny & Joon	1993/98	20s	Lovers / Siblings	Realizing Dreams	Separating	Mental Abilities
(film icon)	Bossa Nova	2000/95	40s	Lovers		Divorce	
(film icon)	Bridget Jones' Diary	2001/97	30s	Lovers			
(film icons)	Can't Buy Me Love	1987/94	Teens	Lovers / Friends / Self-Esteem	Realizing Dreams	Courting	Class Prejudice
(film icons)	Chances Are	1989/108	20s Radical Age Difference	Lovers / Parent/Child		Losing Mate	Loss
(film icons)	Clueless	1995/113	Teens	Lovers / Parent/Child		Courting	Class Prejudice

After-View Feeling Key: Happy   Uplifted   Inspired   Thrilled   Sad

Movie Guide to Romantic Comedies

After-View Feeling	Movie Title	Date/Run Time	Finding Love	Relationships	Work & Prosperity	Transitions	Overcoming Obstacles
	Crossing Delancy	1988/97	30s	Lovers Multi-Generational Family		Courting	Class Prejudice
	Cutting Edge, The	1992/101	20s	Lovers	Realizing Dreams	Courting	
	Dan in Real Life	2007/98	40s	Lovers Multi-Generational Family	Realizing Dreams	Courting	Loss
	Dave	1993/110	40s	Lovers Co-Workers	Loving Your Work	Courting	Class Prejudice
	Definitely, Maybe	2008/112	30s	Lovers Parent/Child		Divorcing	
	Desperately Seeking Susan	1985/103	30s	Friends Lover		Courting Marrying	Entrapment Loss
	Don Juan de Marco	1995/92	60s	Husband/Wife	Realizing Dreams	Retiring	Mental Abilities

After-View Feeling	Movie Title	Date/Run Time	Finding Love	Relationships	Work & Prosperity	Transitions	Overcoming Obstacles
	Emma	1996/120	20s	Friends Lovers		Courting	
	Enchanted	2007/107	30s	Lovers		Courting	Physical Abilities
	Eternal Sunshine of the Spotless Mind	2004/108	30s	Lovers		Separating	Loss
	Ever After	1998/121	20s	Lovers			Class Prejudice
	Fast Times at Ridgemont High	1982/90	Teens	Lovers		Courting	
	Forgetting Sarah Marshall	2008/111	30s	Lovers		Moving Out/Separating	Loss
	Four Weddings and a Funeral	1994/117	30s	Friends Lovers		Courting Marrying	Entrapment Loss

After-View Feeling Key: Happy   Uplifted   Inspired   Thrilled   Sad

Movie Guide to Romantic Comedies

After-View Feeling	Movie Title	Date/Run Time	Finding Love	Relationships	Work & Prosperity	Transitions	Overcoming Obstacles
	Green Card	1991/108	30s	Married Couples	Realizing Dreams	Marrying	
	Greenfingers	2000/91	30s	Boss/Employee Lovers	Loving Your Work	Changing Careers	Creative Expression Entrapment
	Guess Who	2005/105	20s	Fiancé			Getting Married	Racial Prejudice
	Harold and Maude	1971/91	Radical Age Difference	Lovers			Age Prejudice
	High Fidelity	2000/113	30s	Lovers		Moving Out/Separating	
	Hitch	2005/118	30s	Lovers	Loving Your Work	Courting	
	Holiday	1938/93	30s	Lovers Siblings		Changing Careers	Class Prejudice Entrapment
	Holiday, The	2006/138	30s	Lovers		Courting	Entrapment

After-View Feeling	Movie Title	Date/Run Time	Finding Love	Relationships	Work & Prosperity	Transitions	Overcoming Obstacles
Happy	How to Lose a Guy in 10 Days	2003/116	30s	Lovers		Courting	
Happy	I Was a Male War Bride	1949/105	30s	Married Couples		Marrying	
Happy	Impromptu	1991/107	30s	Lovers	Loving Your Work		Creative Expression
Happy	In the Good Old Summertime	1949/102	20s	Lovers			
Happy / Happy	Irreconcilable Differences	1984/112	20s 30s	Parent/Child Two-Career Couples	Balancing Work & Family	Changing Careers Divorcing	Loss
Happy / Happy	It Happened One Night	1934/105	20s	Parent/Child Lovers	Marrying Separating		Class Prejudice Entrapment
Happy	Knight's Tale, A	2001/132	20s	Friends	Realizing Dreams	Changing Careers	Class Prejudice

After-View Feeling Key:

Happy   Uplifted   Inspired   Thrilled   Sad

Movie Guide to Romantic Comedies

After-View Feeling	Movie Title	Date/Run Time	Finding Love	Relationships	Work & Prosperity	Transitions	Overcoming Obstacles
🙂	L.A. Story	1991/95	30s	Lovers		Courting	
🙂	Lonely Hearts	1982/106	30s	Lovers		Courting	
🙂 🙁	Love Actually	2003/135	20s 30s 40s	Lovers Married Couples Parent/Child		Marrying Losing Mate	
🙁 🙂	Love Affair 1939	1939/87	30s	Lovers			
🙂	Love Affair 1994	1994/108	30s	Lovers			
🙂 🙂	Making Mr. Right	1987/95	30s	Co-Workers Lovers	Loving Your Work		Creative Expression
🙂	Matchmaker	1997/97	30s	Lovers	Balancing Work & Family	Courting	
🙂	Me Myself I	1999/104	30s	Lovers		Courting	

After-View Feeling	Movie Title	Date/Run Time	Finding Love	Relationships	Work & Prosperity	Transitions	Overcoming Obstacles
	Mississippi Masala	1992/118	20s	Parent/Child Lovers	Realizing Dreams	Moving Out/ Separating	Racial Prejudice Cultural Abilities
	Month by the Lake, A	1995/91	40s	Lovers		Courting	Age Prejudice
	Much Ado About Nothing	1993/111	30s Teen	Lovers		Courting Marrying	
	Muriel's Wedding	1995/106	20s	Lovers		Courting	
	Murphy's Romance	1986/107	Radical Age Difference	Lovers		Courting	
	Music and Lyrics	2007/96	30s	Lovers	Realizing Dreams	Courting	Loss Creative Expression

After-View Feeling Key: Happy   Uplifted   Inspired   Thrilled   Sad

Movie Guide to Romantic Comedies

After-View Feeling	Movie Title	Date/Run Time	Finding Love	Relationships	Work & Prosperity	Transitions	Overcoming Obstacles
	My Best Friend's Wedding	1997/105	30s	Friends		Courting	
	My Big Fat Greek Wedding	2002/95	30s	Lovers		Courting	Class Prejudice
	Mystic Pizza	1988/101	College Years	Friends Lovers	Realizing Dreams	Moving Out/ Separating	Class Prejudice Entrapment
	Next Stop Wonderland	1998/104	30s	Lovers		Courting	Loss
	Notting Hill	1999/124	30s	Lovers			Class Obstacles
	Peter's Friends	1992/100	30s	Lovers Married Couples	Realizing Dreams	Midlife Crisis	Creative Expression Loss
	Philadelphia Story, The	1940/112	30s	Married Couples		Marrying	
	Pillow Talk	1959/102	30s	Lovers		Courting	

After-View Feeling	Movie Title	Date/Run Time	Finding Love	Relationships	Work & Prosperity	Transitions	Overcoming Obstacles
	Pretty Woman	1990/119	20s 40s	Lovers		Courting	Class Prejudice
	Pride and Prejudice 1995	1995/300	20s	Lovers		Courting	
	Pride and Prejudice 2005	2005/127	20s	Lovers		Courting	
	Romancing the Stone	1984/106	30s	Lovers		Courting	
	Room With a View, A	1986/117	20s	Lovers	Realizing Dreams	Marrying	Entrapment Class Prejudice
	Sense and Sensibility	1995/135	20s	Lovers/Siblings		Courting	Entrapment Class Prejudice
	Shakespeare in Love	1999/123	20s	Lovers		Marrying	Creative Expression

After-View Feeling Key: Happy   Uplifted   Inspired   Thrilled   Sad

After-View Feeling	Movie Title	Date/Run Time	Finding Love	Relationships	Work & Prosperity	Transitions	Overcoming Obstacles
🙂🙂	**She's the One**	1996/95	20s 50s	Lovers Multi-Generational Family Married Couples		Courting	Entrapment
🙂	**Shop Around the Corner, The**	1940/99	20s	Lovers		Courting	
🙂	**Shrek**	2001/108	30s	Lovers			Class Prejudice
😕🙂	**Sideways**	2005/126	40s	Friends Lovers		Marrying	
😕🙂🙂	**Sleepless in Seattle**	1993/104	30s	Lovers		Losing Mate Courting	Loss
🙂🙂	**Some Like It Hot**	1959/119	30s	Co-Workers Lovers	Collaborating w/ Colleagues	Courting	Sexual Prejudice Entrapment

After-View Feeling	Movie Title	Date/Run Time	Finding Love	Relationships	Work & Prosperity	Transitions	Overcoming Obstacles
	Something New	2006/100	30s	Lovers	Realizing Dreams	Achieving Career Goals, Courting	Racial Prejudice, Class Prejudice
	Something to Talk About	1995/106	30s	Married Couples, Multi-Generational Family	Balancing Work & Family	Achieving Career Goals	Entrapment
	Starting Over	1979/106	30s	Lovers, Divorced Couples		Courting, Divorcing	Loss
	Strictly Ballroom	1992/94	20s	Lovers, Parent/Child	Realizing Dreams, Loving Your Work	Courting, Achieving Career Goal	Creative Expression, Entrapment
	Sure Thing, The	1985/94	College Years	Lovers		Courting	Entrapment
	Sweet Home Alabama	2002/108	30s	Lovers		Divorcing	

After-View Feeling Key: Happy   Uplifted   Inspired   Thrilled   Sad

Movie Guide to Romantic Comedies

After-View Feeling	Movie Title	Date/Run Time	Finding Love	Relationships	Work & Prosperity	Transitions	Overcoming Obstacles
	Tao of Steve, The	1990/90	30s	Lovers		Courting	
	Terms of Endearment	1983/129	College Years 30s 50s	Lovers Parent/Child		Courting Marrying Losing Mate	Entrapment Loss
	There's Something About Mary	1998/119	Teens 30s	Lovers		Courting	Mental Abilities
	Thomas Crown Affair, The	1999/98	40s	Lovers	Realizing Dreams	Courting	
	Truth About Cats & Dogs, The	1996/97	30s	Lovers Friends		Courting	Entrapment Self-Esteem
	Tune in Tomorrow	1990/90	Radical Age Difference	Boss/Employee Married Couples	Loving Your Work Collaborating w/ Colleagues	Marrying Achieving Career Goals	Creative Expression

After-View Feeling	Movie Title	Date/Run Time	Finding Love	Relationships	Work & Prosperity	Transitions	Overcoming Obstacles
🙂	Twelfth Night	1996/134	20s	Lovers Siblings			Sexual Prejudice
🙂 🙂	Two for the Road	1967/112	College 20s 30s	Husband/Wife		Courting Marrying	Entrapment
🙂 🙂	Waitress	2007/108	30s	Married Couples	Realizing Dreams	Achieving Career Goals	Entrapment
🙂 🙂	Walking and Talking	1996/86	30s	Lovers Friends		Courting Marrying	Entrapment
🙂	Wedding Planner, The	2001/103	30s	Lovers		Marrying	
🙂 🙂	When Harry Met Sally	1986/96	College Years 30s	Lovers Friends		Courting	Entrapment

After-View Feeling Key:

🙂 Happy   🙂 Uplifted   🙂 Inspired   🙂 Thrilled   🙁 Sad

Movie Guide to Romantic Comedies

After-View Feeling	Movie Title	Date/Run Time	Finding Love	Relationships	Work & Prosperity	Transitions	Overcoming Obstacles
☺	While You Were Sleeping	1995/103	30s	Lovers		Courting	
☺	You've Got Mail	1998/119	30s	Lovers	Realizing Dreams De-structuring Workplace	Losing Job Courting	Class Prejudice

13

100 Movie Descriptions

How to Read the Listings

This chapter gives you plot outlines of movies available on DVD or streaming.

Each listing is presented in the format shown below.

Title •-------• 🎬 **Benny & Joon**

After-View Feeling These emoticons •---------• 😊 😐 This is a fascinating study of love, madness and letting
tell you how you'll feel when you've go, made more beguiling by Depp's superb tribute to comedian Buster
finished watching the film Keaton. Auto garage owner Benny (Quinn) supports his talented artist
sibling Joon (Masterson), a schizophrenic who requires daily supervision
and is relatively calm unless she forgets her medication. Benny's poker game
Plot Outline •-------• loss brings the dyslexic Sam (Depp) to live in their spare bedroom. While
Benny, who loves his sister too much and doesn't have a life of his own,
struggles with the decision to place Joon in a group home, she is captivated
by Sam and his Keaton-inspired routines. As the couple slips into love,
Cast •---------• Benny is unable to release her to live a life of her own, uncertain as that
may be. This charming film creates an air of hope that lingers days later,
despite the seemingly downbeat topic. The music elevates the whimsical
mood recalling a simpler time. Sweet!

Release date and **run time** in mimutes •---------• DVD Release/Run Time : 2000/95 minutes
Director •---------• Director : Jeremiah S. Chechik
Cast : Johnny Depp, Mary Stuart Masterson, Aidan Quinn

Life Chnages explored in the film (see •---------• **Laugh & Cry Movie Rating System**
page 14 for the complete list)

Work & Prosperity	>	Realizing Dreams
Relationships	>	Lovers, Siblings
Finding Love	>	20s
Transitions	>	Separating
Overcoming Obstacles	>	Mental Abilities

10 Things I Hate About You

The Bard's *Taming of the Shrew*, high school style, is still a very funny story in this day and age, for any age. This retelling has senior Kat (Stiles) and her hottie sophomore sister Bianca (Oleynik) coping with their divorced Ob/Gyn father's rule that Bianca can't go to the senior prom unless Kat does. Kat swore off dating when her mother left when Kat was 14 and sees no reason to change now. Bianca's lecherous boyfriend Joey pays Patrick (Ledger) to invite Kat to the prom, so he can take Bianca to the dance. And so the high school mating dance begins with Patrick trying to flirt with the skeptical, cool Kat. Eventually, he breaks her down with Paintball dates and an out-there stadium serenade during football practice, much to Bianca's delight. It all culminates at the dance where Kat learns the truth about Patrick, who is now smitten and has to convince Kat of his true feelings. Larry Miller as her befuddled father punctuates the teen drama with a funny dose of reality.

DVD Release/Run Time	:	1999 / 97 minutes
Director	:	Gil Junger
Cast	:	Heath Ledger, Julia Stiles, Larisa Oleynik, Joseph Gordon-Levitt, Larry Miller

Laugh & Cry Movie Rating System

Transitions	>	Courting
Finding Love	>	Teens
Relationships	>	Lovers

About a Boy

This movie is every slacker dude's fantasy of a rich do-nothing lifestyle. Will's (Grant) father wrote a one-hit Christmas song that has supported his yuppie lifestyle without having to work. Lacking ambition, he hangs out in his smart London loft and watches telly between workouts at the gym. Will strikes upon the ultimate lazy man's dating scheme – going to Single Parents Alone Together (SPAT) and faking having a two-year-old son. He's the only guy in the group and the ladies think he's splendid, until they get suspicious when he fails to produce his kid. Enter Marcus (Hoult), a 12-year-old with divorced, suicidal mother Fiona (Collette), from SPAT, who figures out Will's ruse. Needing a break from his mum's daily drama, he starts joining Will for afternoon TV viewing, despite protests. Will becomes more involved in Marcus' life, even coaching him for a school performance of his mother's favorite song, Killing Me Softly. Then Will becomes smitten with Rachel (Weisz), who also has a son Marcus' age, and slowly realizes life may be more than just about a boy.

DVD Release/Run Time	:	2002/101 minutes
Director	:	Chris Weitz, Paul Weitz
Cast	:	Hugh Grant, Toni Collette, Rachel Weisz,
		Nicholas Hoult, Shari Springer Berman, Robert Pulcini

Laugh & Cry Movie Rating System

Relationships	>	Lovers, Parent/Child, Single Parent
Finding Love	>	30s
Overcoming Obstacles	>	Loss

American Splendor

In a class by itself, this delightful romantic mash-up of documentary footage of real-life graphic novelist couple Harvey Pekar and Joyce Brabner, Harvey's appearances on David Letterman, and their comic book graphics, is interspersed with fictional portrayals by Paul Giamatti and Hope Davis. It tells the story of Harvey and Joyce's quickie romance and the ups and downs of their sometimes happily-ever-after marriage and creative collaboration. A file clerk at the VA Hospital in Cleveland, curmudgeon everyman Harvey creates stick figure comics about his everyday existence, which comic artists like R. Crumb turn into finished drawings. Joyce, owner of a comic book store in Delaware, who knew Harvey's work, meets and marries him in a whirlwind. She then proceeds to propel him on a new career path that includes merchandising and a graphic novel about his experience with cancer. This true-life comedy shows the value of a prickly partnership of equals in the best Hepburn-Tracy tradition.

DVD Release/Run Time	:	2003/101 minutes
Director	:	Shari Springer Berman, Robert Pulcini
Cast	:	Paul Giamatti, Hope Davis, Harvey Pekar, Joyce Brabner

Laugh & Cry Movie Rating System

Work & Prosperity	>	Realizing Dreams
Relationships	>	Married Couples
Finding Love	>	50s
Transitions	>	Marrying
Overcoming Obstacles	>	Creative Expression

An Affair To Remember

Director Leo McCarey's second remake of his classic tearjerker stars Cary Grant as British playboy painter Nicky Farrante and Deborah Kerr as singer Terry McKay. It's a shipboard romance between two people who are "supported" by their respective fiancés. When Nicky takes Kay to visit his grandmother (Nesbitt) at the ship's stop in Madeira, you can feel the deliciousness of their flirtation deepening into a lasting love. The couple agrees to meet in six months at the top of the Empire State Building while each figures out how to earn a living. On the way to the meeting, Terry has a terrible taxicab accident that leaves her unable to walk. She refuses to tell Nicky what happened. He eventually tracks her down in her NY apartment at Christmas time in the three-hanky finale to be remembered for all time. Originally made in 1932 and referenced in *Sleepless in Seattle*, this story has been remade for every generation: *Love Affair* (1939) with Charles Boyer and Janet Gaynor and *Love Affair* (1994) with husband-wife team Warren Beatty and Annette Benning. Maybe it's time for a 21st century update, this time with texting and twittering. Nancy Meyers, how about it?

DVD Release/Run Time	:	1957/119 minutes
Director	:	Leo McCarey
Cast	:	Cary Grant, Deborah Kerr, Cathleen Nesbitt

Laugh & Cry Movie Rating System

Relationships	>	Lovers
Finding Love	>	30s
Overcoming Obstacles	>	Breaking Old Patterns

Annie Hall

With *Annie Hall*, Woody Allen revived the romantic comedy genre for a new generation, which had languished in the turmoil of the 60s. He plays Alvy Singer, a New York theater director, who becomes involved with Annie Hall (Keaton), a singer. She is a perfect match for his angst, but wrong for him in every other respect, creating lots of laugh-out-loud situations. His fear of commitment and losing control ultimately encages him in an even more fearful place of isolated loneliness. This is a very funny and awfully sad look at the truth of making a relationship work: You have to start with the right partner and not be afraid to enjoy the journey. Allen's comedy is definitely an acquired taste based on his neurotic nebbish New Yorker denial that he is the creator of his life's choices. If you enjoy the Allen touch, this film is one of his best. It received five Oscar nominations and won for Best Director, Best Screenplay, and Best Actress.

DVD Release/Run Time	:	1977/95 minutes
Director	:	Woody Allen
Cast	:	Woody Allen, Diane Keaton, Tony Roberts

Laugh & Cry Movie Rating System

Relationships	>	Lovers
Finding Love	>	30s
Overcoming Obstacles	>	Breaking Old Patterns

The Awful Truth

Happy, wealthy married couple Jerry and Lucy Warriner (Grant and Dunne) have a series of unfortunate misunderstandings that spiral into unfortunate divorce proceedings. As the final divorce draws near, each starts meddling in the other's romance. Awkward, amusing situations abound, like when Lucy poses as Jerry's scandalous sister at his first meeting with his fiancé's parents. Or when Grant drops by Dunne's apartment to visit their dog (he got visitation rights), her clueless oil man fiancé (Bellamy) tries to get a first kiss from her, while a bemused Grant hides behind the front door. The awful truth is that they are still crazy about each other, but each is too adamant to admit it. This is great screwball comedy at its best by director Leo McCarey (*An Affair to Remember*), who won the Best Director Oscar. What is unintentionally laughable today are Dunne's ridiculous outfits and hairstyles, but somehow it only heightens the film's silliness. This funny classic was voted one of the 50 best all-time comedies by *Premiere* magazine.

DVD Release/Run Time	:	1937/91 minutes
Director	:	Leo McCarey
Cast	:	Cary Grant, Irene Dunne, Ralph Bellamy

Laugh & Cry Movie Rating System

Relationships	>	Married Couples
Finding Love	>	30s
Transitions	>	Divorcing

Barcelona

Set in anti-America Barcelona after Franco's downfall in the early 80s, this quirky romance of culture clash is about two bickering cousins, an uptight American salesman Ted Boynton (Nichols) and a slightly less inhibited U.S. Naval officer Fred Boynton (Eigeman), who court sexually aggressive young Spanish women unleashing two generations of pent up sexual, political, and artistic repression. Ted can't get rid of Fred, who operates in an oblivious cloud of arrogant American naiveté. Part of the fun is the Spanish blindness that makes this military jerk irresistible to the senoritas in Barcelona because he is American, but he's still an impossible dweeb who has a hard time getting a date at home. Clever and enjoyable, this underrated indie captures the right 80s disco tone and manner a la Espana and helps you understand both the Spanish and the American perspectives in a most amusing way. Ole!

DVD Release/Run Time	:	1994/102 minutes
Director	:	Whit Stillman
Cast	:	Taylor Nichols, Chris Eigeman, Tuska Bergen, Mira Sorvino

Laugh & Cry Movie Rating System

Work & Prosperity	>	Realizing Dreams
Relationships	>	Lovers
Finding Love	>	20s
Transitions	>	Courting
Overcoming Obstacles	>	Cultural Abilities

Beautiful Girls

Once every so often, the lightning of the confusing, conflicting, congealing emotions needed to grow up is captured in the clear bottle of an ensemble film that asks the question: Is a beautiful girl as good as love? *Beautiful Girls* brings together the best actors of their day in an entertaining story that perfectly captures the jump-shift passage from the commitment-phobe 20s into 30s adulthood. Set in a small town in Wisconsin, it looks at those who leave for Chicago, like engaged piano player Willie (Hutton) and lovely Andrea (Thurman), and those who stay to numb themselves with alcohol and supermodel fantasies, and the patient women who love them, even though the women know they can never measure up. Three of the men (Dillon, Rapaport, Perlich) scrape by operating a snow removal business while they rate women on a scale from 1 to 10, play immature games with their women's affections, and start to realize that this is not where they thought their lives would end up at age 30. Gina (O'Donnell) shines as the single cynic who nails the dilemma their dreams have created amidst the doldrums of their everyday life.

DVD Release/Run Time	:	1996/110 minutes
Director	:	Ted Demme
Cast	:	Timothy Hutton, Annabeth Gish, Matt Dillon, Lauren Holly, Michael Rapaport, Rosie O'Donnell, Uma Thurman, Martha Plimpton, Mira Sorvino, Natalie Portman

Laugh & Cry Movie Rating System

Work & Prosperity	>	Realizing Dreams
Relationships	>	Lovers, Friends
Finding Love	>	30s
Transitions	>	20s to 30s Passage
Overcoming Obstacles	>	Entrapment

Bend It Like Beckham

Here's a charming movie that stirs up warm-hearted fun with immigrant tradition and the generation gap in 21st century London. It's a very funny tale of a Sikh teenager, Jess (Nagra), juggling dreams of soccer fame, a crush on David Beckham, and refugee parents who want her to cook a good Punjabi dinner and become a lawyer. When an English girl, Jules (Knightley) invites her to try out for a girl's soccer team, Jess doesn't even know there is such a thing. She and Jules eventually break over their cute soccer coach's affections. When an American university coach with scholarships wants to see them play, the game conflicts with Jess' sister's wedding. Jess is not the only teen with a mother who just doesn't understand. Jules' mother, a proper English clothing storeowner and fashionista, has visions of a no-grandchild future when she believes her only child is gay. As Jules straightens her out, the mother does some priceless backpedaling. A rocking feel-good score fuses Indian and R&B music to punctuate the hilarity and kick the action on the soccer field toward the goal. Even the DVD extras are amusing. Be sure to watch how to cook Punjabi aloo gobi with the director and her aunties bantering over the best combination of ingredients.

DVD Release/Run Time	:	2003/112 minutes
Director	:	Gurinder Chadha
Cast	:	Paraminder Nagra, Keira Knightley,
		Jonathon Rhys-Meyers

Laugh & Cry Movie Rating System

Work & Prosperity	>	Realizing Dreams
Relationships	>	Lovers, Parent/Child
Finding Love	>	Teen Years
Overcoming Obstacles	>	Racial Prejudice

Benny & Joon

This is a fascinating study of love, madness and letting go, made more beguiling by Depp's superb tribute to comedian Buster Keaton. Auto garage owner Benny (Quinn) supports his talented artist sibling Joon (Masterson), a schizophrenic who requires daily supervision and is relatively calm unless she forgets her medication. Benny's poker game loss brings the dyslexic Sam (Depp) to live in their spare bedroom. While Benny, who loves his sister too much and doesn't have a life of his own, struggles with the decision to place Joon in a group home, she is captivated by Sam and his Keaton-inspired routines. As the couple slips into love, Benny is unable to release her to live a life of her own, uncertain as that may be. This charming film creates an air of hope that lingers days later, despite the seemingly downbeat topic. The music elevates the whimsical mood recalling a simpler time. Sweet!

DVD Release/Run Time	:	2000/95 minutes
Director	:	Jeremiah S. Chechik
Cast	:	Johnny Depp, Mary Stuart Masterson, Aidan Quinn

Laugh & Cry Movie Rating System

Work & Prosperity	>	Realizing Dreams
Relationships	>	Lovers, Siblings
Finding Love	>	20s
Transitions	>	Separating
Overcoming Obstacles	>	Mental Abilities

Bossa Nova

Direct from the beaches of Rio, this Brazilian comedy is a hot sexy romance for the Boomer crowd set to the bossa nova beat. Marianne (Irving) is an attractive 40something American widow who teaches English and attracts students who are always making awkward passes at her. There's the handsome lawyer Pedro Paulo (Fagundes), divorcing his travel agent wife, who literally runs into Marianne in their office building elevator. Pedro immediately decides he needs to take English lessons from her. Then there is the Brazilian soccer star who has just signed a contract with an English team. Throw in the fact that Pedro is working on his father's divorce. All sorts of screwball entanglements keep the plot rollicking along. The sensual score keeps the mood light and breezy with spectacular Rio cinematography you don't have to get on a plane to enjoy. It's a real treat to see people in their 40s and 50s portrayed as romantic leads. Why are American couples over 40 rarely shown in sexy situations? Well, except maybe for those male enhancement ads.

DVD Release/Run Time	:	2000/95 minutes
Director	:	Bruno Barreto
Cast	:	Amy Irving, Antonio Fagundes

Laugh & Cry Movie Rating System

Relationships	>	Lovers
Finding Love	>	40s
Transitions	>	Divorce

Bridget Jones' Diary

Think Elizabeth Bennett reincarnated as a neurotic but loveable modern day Londoner named Bridget Jones (a 20 pounds heavier Zellweger). She's single and dedicated to improving herself in one year by diligently tracking in her daily diary her weight and the number of cigarettes smoked. All this discipline is focused on finding a suitable mate. In the meantime, she overeats, drinks too much, and stays in a going-nowhere relationship with her cad of a boss (Grant). None of this does much for her pudgy self's esteem. At her parents' Christmas party, she reconnects with her childhood friend, lawyer Mark Darcy (Firth) amidst her parents' acrimonious separation. Now, in addition to her own disappointing dating life, she has to listen to her morose father complain while her mother is off having a divine time with her new boyfriend. Amusingly, Bridget rallies her strength to quit her publishing job and her boss for a TV commentator position where she gets herself into another round of hilarious situations, this time on-air. Her friendship with Mr. Darcy lands her a big scoop from one of his clients. I wonder what Jane Austen would have to say about the brawl in the end. Is this how gentlemen behave in the presence of a lady? Mmmm.

DVD Release/Run Time	:	2001/97 minutes
Director	:	Sharon Maguire
Cast	:	Renee Zellweger, Colin Firth, Hugh Grant

Laugh & Cry Movie Rating System

Relationships	>	Lovers
Finding Love	>	30s

Can't Buy Me Love

Long before he was Dr. McDreamy, Patrick Dempsey was Ronald Miller, the geeky lawn boy who wants desperately to be accepted by the "in" crowd at his Tucson high school in this delightful 80s teen classic. When wealthy head cheerleader Cindy Mancini (Peterson) ruins her mother's $1000 suede dress, Ronald decides to buy her a new one if she agrees to spend time with him for one month. The ploy works for a while, especially after Cindy does a makeover on Ronald. But he's not prepared for how much he likes hanging out with his cool new friends, turning a blind eye to the fact that Cindy is starting to enjoy being with him. Ronald's transformation – from nerd to popular man-about-campus back to social outcast before he ultimately finds self-acceptance – is entertaining to watch. It's not a new story – the rich cheerleader with big 80s hair falling for the made-over geek has been done before. But this film stands out as one of the first and the best because the chemistry between Dempsey and Peterson is so convincing and undeniably appealing every time you watch it, and, just guessing here, you will want to see it more than once.

DVD Release/Run Time	:	1987/94 minutes
Director	:	Steve Rash
Cast	:	Amanda Peterson, Patrick Dempsey

Laugh & Cry Movie Rating System

Work & Prosperity	>	Realizing Dreams
Relationships	>	Lovers, Friends, Self-Esteem
Finding Love	>	Teen Years
Transitions	>	Courting
Overcoming Obstacles	>	Class Prejudice

Chances Are

This is a wonderful, witty, ironic fantasy about a young widow, Corrine Jefferies (Shepherd at her best), who finds herself pregnant after her husband Louie (McDonald) is killed in a car crash. In heaven, Louie negotiates a return to earth pleading he was too young to die, but he must wait to come back as his daughter's boyfriend Alex Finch (a young and always great Downey). Fast forward 20 years, when Louie returns home in Alex's body with his daughter/girlfriend Miranda (Masterson) and slowly starts to remember the passion he had for Corrine. Now he's torn by his feelings for both women. You can guess where this is going, but the comic chemistry between Corrine and Alex sizzles and convinces you to join in on the fun. This underrated romantic comedy is directed by comic master Emile Ardolino, who brought you *Dirty Dancing* and *Sister Act*.

DVD Release/Run Time	:	1989/108 minutes
Director	:	Emile Ardolino
Cast	:	Cybill Shepherd, Robert Downey, Jr., Ryan O'Neal, Mary Stuart Masterson, Christopher McDonald

Laugh & Cry Movie Rating System

Relationships	>	Lovers, Parent/Child
Finding Love	>	20s, Radical Age Difference
Transitions	>	Losing Mate
Overcoming Obstacles	>	Loss

Clueless

Way before Paris Hilton hit the scene, this hilarious satire of our fashionista culture tells the teenage adventures of Cher Horowitz (Silverstone), a nouveau rich, spoiled brat at Beverly Hills High. Daughter of a high-powered attorney (Hedaya), Cher has more stuff than sense as she caroms around Beverly Hills with her best friend Dionne (Dash) in her trendsetting outfits and fancy cars. Cher can't resist making over lost soul classmate Tai (Murphy), a New York newcomer, and proceeds to set her up with a series of disastrous dates. Meanwhile, Cher is going out with Christian (Walker) who shares her passion for style, but not anything more, and Cher can't seem to understand why. Only her skeptical stepbrother Josh (Rudd) can call her bluff, but he eventually succumbs to her charms as well. This film was made when Silverstone was at the height of her Teen Choice Award popularity. The movie wardrobe set the fashion standards for a whole new generation of teen and tween girls including, just guessing, Paris herself. Compare *Clueless* with *Emma*, starring Gwyneth Paltrow, the original Jane Austen story set in early 19th century rural England. But it's, like, way more fun retold with late 20th century Beverly Hills attitude and outfits.

DVD Release / Run Time	:	1995 / 113 minutes
Director	:	Amy Heckerling
Cast	:	Alicia Silverstone, Stacey Dash, Paul Rudd, Brittany Murphy, Dan Hedaya, Justin Walker

Laugh & Cry Movie Rating System

Relationships	>	Lovers, Parent/Child
Finding Love	>	Teen Years
Transitions	>	Courting
Overcoming Obstacles	>	Class Prejudice

Corrina, Corrina

Set to the cool tunes of 1950s jazz classics like Louis Armstrong's "You Go To My Head," a black musicologist Corrina Washington (Goldberg), working as a housekeeper to make ends meet, draws out grieving little white girl Molly Singer (Majorino), who has refused to speak since her mother's death. To his daughter's delight, a romance starts to unfold between Corrina and her music jingle-writing father Manny Singer (Liotta). When Corrina helps Manny solve a musical bridge problem for a Mr. Potato Head advertising jingle, he starts listening to her aspirations to write liner notes for jazz albums and views her in a whole new light. Of course, it's the 50s and both their families have strong interracial objections to the match. But love for each other, Molly, and music triumph in the end. This is a rare and moving examination of loss, grieving, and healing, told from a child's perspective. Check out the wonderful soundtrack CD to keep that 50s jazz and R&B vibe going.

DVD Release/Run Time	:	1994/115 minutes
Director	:	Jessie Nelson
Cast	:	Whoopi Goldberg, Ray Liotta, Tina Majorino

Laugh & Cry Movie Rating System

Relationships	>	Lovers, Parent/Child
Finding Love	>	30s
Transitions	>	Courting, Losing Mate
Overcoming Obstacles	>	Loss, Racial Prejudice

Crossing Delancy

This is a wry and wistful story of a 30-something Manhattan Jewish bookworm Izzy Grossman (Irving) learning to find love through her heart, not her head. Her so-called intellectually perfect life starts to unravel when her old country grandmother Bubbe Kantor (the splendid Bozyk), concerned about Izzy's spinsterhood, takes matters in her own hand and hires a Lower East Side Jewish matchmaker, the hilarious Hannah Mandelbaum (Miles). Hannah offers up a big-hearted Delancy Street pickle store heir Sam Posner (Reigert). But Izzy's not so sure she wants to look in lower Manhattan for a date, let alone a husband. Izzy does agree to go to dinner with Sam, just to humor Bubbe. Sam is smitten and starts wooing Izzy with gifts and wise stories. Still uncertain, Izzy fixes Sam up with a friend of hers. She clings to her fantasy about working with famous author Anton Maes (Krabbe). But when Anton makes it clear that he really just needs a secretary, she runs back to Bubbe's apartment hoping it's not too late to catch Sam. Maybe Bubbe does know best after all. Irving's performance was nominated for a Golden Globe Best Actress award.

DVD Release/Run Time	:	1988/97 minutes
Director	:	Joan Micklin Silver
Cast	:	Amy Irving, Reizl Bozyk, Peter Riegert, Jeroen Krabbé, Sylvia Miles

Laugh & Cry Movie Rating System

Relationships	>	Lovers, Multi-Generational Family
Finding Love	>	30s
Transitions	>	Courting
Overcoming Obstacles	>	Class Prejudice

The Cutting Edge

Take Doug Dorsey (Sweeny), a rough and tumble Minnesota Olympic college hockey player with an eye injury, and pair him with spoiled, ambitious Connecticut Olympic pairs figure skater Kate Moseley (Kelly), who can't keep a partner, and watch the sparks fly as they fight, bicker, and banter about how to go for the Olympic Gold together under the stern guidance of a Russian pairs coach. This is an engaging look at the taming of the sexy ruffian and the thawing of the Ice Queen set against the grind and suspense of competitive pairs skating, with a smart script from the award-winning scribe Tony Gilroy (the *Bourne* series, *Michael Clayton*, *The Devil's Advocate*) that stands the test of time. You leave feeling happy and perhaps hopeful that the competitive bickering of Kate and Doug may eventually mellow into happily ever after. The story has continued into the next generation in two recent TV movie sequels, with *Cutting Edge 2* also written by Gilroy.

DVD Release/Run Time	:	1992/101 minutes
Director	:	Paul Michael Glaser
Cast	:	D.B. Sweeny, Moira Kelly

Laugh & Cry Movie Rating System

Work & Prosperity	>	Realizing Dreams
Relationships	>	Lovers
Finding Love	>	20s
Transitions	>	Courting

Dan in Real Life

What's Dan (Carell), parenting columnist and widower with three daughters, to do when he inadvertently falls for his brother's girlfriend Marie (Binoche) at a large family gathering held at his parents' Rhode Island summer home? Still grieving for his wife after four years, Dan gets lots of unsolicited dating advice from his well-meaning but annoying family members. Then Dan has a chance meeting with an intriguing lady in a bookstore that ignites instant chemistry. Try as Dan may to mask the awkward attraction from the family, he's busted by his teenage daughters, who know a thing or two about flirting. This sweet, funny, multi-generational comedy is a 21st century update in the *Parenthood* tradition, with all the endearing, enraging, and enduring emotions that challenge any parent attempting to develop a loving adult relationship without mimicking the teenage antics and operatic angst of his children. In real life, you just have to plan to be surprised.

DVD Release/Run Time	:	2007/98 minutes
Director	:	Peter Hedges
Cast	:	Steve Carell, Juliette Binoche, Dane Cook, Allison Pill, Dianne Weist

Laugh & Cry Movie Rating System

Work & Prosperity	>	Realizing Dreams
Relationships	>	Lovers, Multi-Generational Family
Finding Love	>	40s
Transitions	>	Courting
Overcoming Obstacles	>	Loss

Dave

Before Barack Obama put his community organizing skills to work to get elected president, this film offered a refreshing, upbeat tale of ordinary nice guy Dave Kovic (Klein), a Presidential look-alike who is thrust into permanently posing as the chief of state, when the real president Bill Mitchell is felled by a debilitating stroke. As a Washington, DC temporary staffing agency owner, Dave knows how to put people to work. Trouble begins when Dave starts to enjoy his new job and employ his talents, to the horror of the Haig-like White House Chief of Staff Bob Alexander (Langella). Dave even brings in his own CPA Murray Blum (Grodin) to a Cabinet meeting to help balance the federal budget with uproarious results. Dave finds money for the First Lady's pet children's project in the exercise. With intelligent tenderness, a romance between the neglected President's wife Ellen (Weaver) and Dave blossoms as White House intrigue to dethrone him escalates. Enjoy this endearing comedy whenever you want to revive your hope that nice guys can get the girl and have an impact on the government for the good of all the people.

DVD Release/Run Time	:	1993/110 minutes
Director	:	Ivan Reitman
Cast	:	Kevin Kline, Sigourney Weaver, Frank Langella, Charles Grodin

Laugh & Cry Movie Rating System

Work & Prosperity	>	Loving Your Work
Relationships	>	Lovers, Co-Workers
Finding Love	>	40s
Transitions	>	Courting
Overcoming Obstacles	>	Class Prejudice

Definitely, Maybe

This clever romance is presented as a mystery told by 30-something divorcing dad Will Hayes (Reynolds) to his insistent 10-year-old daughter Maya (Breslin), who wants to know the truth about how he fell in love with her mother. Over the course of several evenings, Will tells her the bedtime stories of the three loves in his life, tantalizing Maya to guess which one is her mother. Is she his college sweetheart (Banks) who is reluctant to move from Wisconsin to New York with him when he was an idealistic Clinton political worker? Or is it his best friend-buddy and confidante (Fisher)? Perhaps it's the free-spirited, ambitious journalist (Weisz)? Maybe you can guess the answer. Otherwise, you'll just have to see the flick to find out. It's a touching tale that will definitely leave you feeling uplifted.

DVD Release/Run Time	:	2008/112 minutes
Director	:	Adam Brooks
Cast	:	Ryan Reynolds, Abigail Breslin, Elizabeth Banks, Isla Fisher, Rachel Weisz

Laugh & Cry Movie Rating System

Relationships	>	Lovers, Parent/Child
Finding Love	>	30s
Transitions	>	Divorcing

Desperately Seeking Susan

In this "I love the 80s" screwball comedy of mistaken identity and culture clash, bored, young, Jewish, Fort Lee, NJ housewife Roberta Glass (Arquette), whose strait-laced husband Gary operates a prosperous hot tub business, seeks adventure by responding to a NYC classified ad seeking Susan (Madonna). Roberta runs away from her husband, assumes Susan's identity, and jumps into the exciting NYC punk rock world, filled with kooky characters. She takes a job as a magician's assistant and tries to evade a mob hit man in pursuit of the real Susan. Dez (Quinn), a friend of Susan's rocker boyfriend, takes pity on Roberta/Susan and invites her to crash at his place, which leads to much more. With more plot reverses than it takes to get out of a tight parking spot, this cheerful film caroms along and invites you for a fun-filled ride. Check out Madonna at the height of her trendsetting *Like a Virgin* fame, and arguably in her best movie role – playing herself.

DVD Release/Run Time	:	1985/103 minutes
Director	:	Susan Seidelman
Cast	:	Rosanne Arquette, Aiden Quinn, Madonna

Laugh & Cry Movie Rating System

Relationships	>	Friends, Lovers
Finding Love	>	30s
Transitions	>	Courting, Marrying
Overcoming Obstacles	>	Entrapment, Loss

Don Juan de Marco

This is a thoroughly charming tale of the power of romance to heal pain and a mental patient's romantic fantasies to cure his psychiatrist's cold heart. An imaginative, though suicidal, young man calling himself Don Juan de Marco (Depp), posing as the world's greatest lover, enchants psychiatrist Dr. Jack Mickler (Brando) with his tales of courtship and seduction. The doctor is attempting to heal Don Juan in just 10 days before he retires. Transfixed by the sagas of love, Dr. Mickler begins to see ways he might enliven his own comfortable marriage. To watch his wife Marilyn's (Dunaway) response to her husband's surprising seduction is to revive hope for keeping the flames of love alive long after so-called retirement. Listing Lord Byron as a co-writer, writer/director Leven provides a delightful stage for three wonderful actors to show their best stuff.

DVD Release/Run Tim	:	1995/92 minutes
Director	:	Jeremy Leven
Cast	:	Marlon Brando, Johnny Depp, Faye Dunaway

Laugh & Cry Movie Rating System

Work & Prosperity	>	Realizing Dreams
Relationships	>	Husband/Wife
Finding Love	>	60s
Transitions	>	Retiring
Overcoming Obstacles	>	Mental Abilities

Emma

Emma Woodhouse, handsome, clever, and rich, with a comfortable home and happy disposition, is the focus of Jane Austen's keen, satirical eye for the foibles of the English rural upper class in the early 1800s. Austen's ear for witty, upbeat dialogue translates very well into this screen version of the tale of 21-year-old Emma (Paltrow), a girl who can't resist making over and matching up poor Harriet Smith (Collette), a girl of questionable origin, in a series of disastrous fix ups over the course of one year. Emma dotes on her silly elderly hypochondriac father while being completely blind to her own shortcomings and insensitive to the position and plight of others less fortunate. Emma's brother-in-law, the dashing Mr. Knightley (Northam), 16 years her senior, watches her antics with cynicism, then exasperation, and finally irresistible attraction. See *Clueless* for a very funny 90s Beverly Hills High School spin on this story.

DVD Release/Run Time	:	1996/120 minutes
Director	:	Douglas McGrath
Cast	:	Gwyneth Paltrow, Jeremy Northam, Greta Scacchi, Toni Collette

Laugh & Cry Movie Rating System

Relationships	>	Friends, Lovers
Finding Love	>	20s
Transitions	>	Courting

Enchanted

This Disney family film starts out like most in their huge animation catalog – a princess named Giselle (Smart) singing to a bevy of animals about her upcoming marriage to the handsome prince named Edward (Marsden). But then it makes a riotous right turn into reality as the prince's wicked stepmother (Sarandon) drops our princess into modern day Manhattan to save the throne for herself. Giselle tries to return to the kingdom through a Palace Casino billboard, but is reluctantly rescued by single lawyer dad Robert (Dempsey). His 6 year old daughter Morgan is, well, enchanted by Giselle and her magical abilities to summon through song an array of animals to clean their messy apartment. Of course, there are complications – what with Robert's long-term girlfriend, who has been waiting five years for him to propose, and Prince Edward arriving looking for his true love. We can guess how it's going to end at a ball, but it's such a pleasurable mash up of animation, live-action musical numbers, family-friendly romantic comedy, and a refreshing, new-found ability for Disney to have fun with itself, at last, after how many generations?

DVD Release/Run Time	:	2007/107 minutes
Director	:	Kevin Lima
Cast	:	Amy Smart, Patrick Dempsey, James Marsden,
		Timothy Spall, Susan Sarandon

Laugh & Cry Movie Rating System

Relationships	>	Lovers
Finding Love	>	30s
Transitions	>	Courting
Overcoming Obstacles	>	Physical Abilities

Eternal Sunshine of the Spotless Mind

What if there was a high tech solution that would make breaking up not so hard to do? This delicious dark sci-fi comedy speculates on what could happen if there is a way to wipe all memory and feeling of a relationship gone awry. Clementine (Winslet) and Joel (Carrey) agree to undergo a radical treatment that will do just that. If you can accept this mind-bending premise, you'll be delighted with the perplexity of Joel's out-of-sequence flashbacks of the various stages of his love for Clementine. It's a merry mystery to figure out where they are in their relationship in each scene. The surprise is Joel's profound sense of loss when the "operation" is complete and what options he has in the end. It's definitely worth a second look, if only to straighten out Clementine's wild hair color changes. Kate Winslet was nominated for a Best Actress Oscar and Charlie Kaufman, director Michel Gondry and Pierre Bismuth won for Best Writing, Original Screenplay.

DVD Release/Run Time	:	2004/108 minutes
Director	:	Michel Gondry
Cast	:	Kate Winslet, Jim Carrey, Elijah Wood, Tom Wilkinson

Laugh & Cry Movie Rating System

Relationships	>	Lovers
Finding Love	>	30s
Transitions	>	Separation
Overcoming Obstacles	>	Loss

Ever After

Beautifully narrated by Jeanne Moreau, she relates the true story about her great-great grandmother and the prince that became the Cinderella fairy tale. This inspired update adds a charming back story with a girl power edge for all the usual suspects – the selfish stepmother, played with bravura by Angela Huston; her two whiny daughters; the handsome, spoiled man-child prince, tutored at the 15th century French court by Leonardo di Vinci; and Cinderella minus the self esteem issues, as enacted by a captivating Drew Barrymore. She's just trying to keep the family estate in tact, despite her stepmother's spendthrift ways. As the relationship with the Prince unfolds, Cinderella even chides him into taking more of an interest in his subjects and set up a university. This movie leaves you with the drifting into the drowsiness feeling of a good bedtime story you love hearing over again, but this time serving up an even better promise – that a match of equals can indeed live happily ever after.

DVD Release/Run Time	:	1998/121 minutes
Director	:	Andy Tennant
Cast	:	Drew Barrymore, Dougray Scott, Angelica Huston

Laugh & Cry Movie Rating System

Relationships	>	Lovers
Finding Love	>	20s
Overcoming Obstacles	>	Class Prejudice

Fast Times at Ridgemont High

Directed by comic master Amy Heckerling (*Clueless*), here's the perfect movie when you feel like a blast from the 80s high school past. This classic raised the teen movie bar with an amusingly honest telling of the issues facing teens of any generation – college prep, fast food jobs, sports, sex, drugs, and rock & roll. Written by Cameron Crowe (*Say Anything*, *Jerry Maguire*), based on his own San Diego high school experience, he created the archetype stoner surfer dude Spiccoli (Penn), who orders pizza delivered to history class, much to the consternation of the clueless martinet teacher Mr. Hand (Walston). It's all there – the fast food jobs in silly uniforms working for inept managers to finance high school fun and the college fund. Then there's the raging hormone boogie of sexual awakening that's good for laughs and cries of pregnancy shame. The stellar young cast includes those who went on to become great actors and directors including Sean Penn, Forest Whitaker, Judge Rheinold, Jennifer Jason Leigh, Phoebe Cates, and a bit part Nicolas Cage.

DVD Release/Run Time	:	1982/90 minutes
Director	:	Amy Heckerling
Cast	:	Sean Penn, Jennifer Jason Leigh, Ray Walston,
		Judge Rheinold, Forest Whitaker, Phoebe Cates

Laugh & Cry Movie Rating System

Relationships	>	Lovers
Finding Love	>	Teens
Transitions	>	Courting

Forgetting Sarah Marshall

Forgetting Sarah Marshall twists the usual romantic comedy setup on its ear by having the guy play the traditional heartbroken girl's role. Composer Peter (Segal) is devastated by the break up with his vapid, self-centered TV-star girlfriend Sarah (Bell). To lick his wounds, Peter takes off to Oahu's North Shore and checks into the very same hotel where Sarah and her new British rocker boyfriend (Brand) are staying. At night, Peter sobs so loudly his neighbors complain. During the day, he has hilarious encounters with a Hawaiian cast of characters. There's the stoner surf shop manager (Rudd) and a weed dealer waiter (*Moneyball's* Hill) who do little to help Peter move past his grief. Sympathetic front desk clerk Rachel (Kunis) does more than upgrade his room by showing Peter other possibilities. This film has lots of laugh-out-loud moments, leaving you with an upbeat feeling that it's possible to feel alive again, even after you've been to the depths of a bad breakup.

DVD Release/Run Time	:	2008/111 minutes
Director	:	Nick Stoller
Cast	:	Jason Segel, Kristen Bell, Mila Kunis, Russell Brand

Laugh & Cry Movie Rating System

Relationships	>	Lovers
Finding Love	>	30s
Transitions	>	Moving Out/Separating
Overcoming Obstacles	>	Loss

Four Weddings and a Funeral

This is an amusing, mirthful look at a group of 30-something upmarket London singles, at a time when all their friends are getting married. Charles (Grant) is a handsome heart-breaker, a confirmed commitment-phobe and a shy closet romantic waiting for the thunderbolt. That changes when he meets Cary (MacDowell), an uninhibited American fashion editor, at the first wedding. After a one-night fling, he's hooked, but endearingly confused about expressing his feelings for her. Each wedding has its charming and hilarious moments. At the second wedding, Charles uncomfortably confronts his past indiscretions when he is seated at a table with several old flames where the ladies proceed to swap Charles stories. Carrie marries an older wealthy Scotsman at the third wedding, but one of Charles' closest friends has a heart attack. As Charles is preparing to be married at the fourth wedding, Carrie shows up without her husband. This film was created by a team of comedy experts. Director Mike Newell (*Enchanted April*) takes the funny, feel-good, uplifting afterglow to new heights. Writer Richard Curtis went on to write and direct *Love Actually*.

DVD Release/Run Time	: 1994/117
Director	: Mike Newell
Cast	: Hugh Grant, Andie MacDowell, Kristen Scott Thomas

Laugh & Cry Movie Rating System

Relationships	>	Friends, Lovers
Finding Love	>	30s
Transitions	>	Courting, Marrying
Overcoming Obstacles	>	Entrapment, Loss

Green Card

This is a delicious romantic comedy about a coldhearted marriage of convenience melting into a fuzzy love affair under the very funny scrutiny of family, friends, and the INS. To obtain a green card, prickly French waiter and aspiring composer Georges (Depardieu) figures he'll marry an American. Attractive American horticulturist Bronte (MacDowell) agrees so she will qualify to buy a NYC co-op that is restricted to married owners and has the perfect room for her dream garden. Neither expects to see the other again after the wedding, but their emotional tango begins when the INS starts asking questions. Forced to move in together, Bronte and Georges have one harried weekend to construct a life together with fake seasonal photos, while memorizing intimate facts about each other. They hope this will convince their skeptical INS officer that they really are a couple. In the rush to outsmart the INS, they start to actually fall in love.

DVD Release/Run Time	:	1991/108 minutes
Director	:	Peter Weir
Cast	:	Gerard Depardieu, Andie MacDowell

Laugh & Cry Movie Rating System

Work & Prosperity	>	Realizing Dreams
Relationships	>	Married Couples
Finding Love	>	30s
Transitions	>	Marrying

Greenfingers

In the U.S., we'd call this film *Green Thumb*. But no matter the digit, based on improbable true events, this British charmer relates how an experimental open prison rehabilitation program taught hardened criminals how to garden as a trade, and ends up revealing a surprising creative talent for flower growing. Add in a talented cast led by Clive Owen and Helen Mirren, and let the droll garden show begin. One very talented gardener (Owens) and his four fellow prison mates find a champion in one of their rehab program advisors – a famous horticulturalist, Georgina Woodhouse, in all her large flowered-hat glory (Mirren). She insists that the prisoners be entered in the Hampton Court Palace Flower Show Garden contest, sponsored by Queen Elizabeth. Very amusing situations arise along the way between the Establishment's expectations of "hardened" criminal behavior and their raw talent channeled into the British national passion for creating exquisite award-winning gardens. Let's not forget the unexpected romance between Georgina's daughter and the gifted hunky gardening genius thrown into the comic compost.

DVD Release/Run Time	:	2000/91 minutes
Director	:	Joel Hershman
Cast	:	Clive Owen, Helen Mirren, David Kelly

Laugh & Cry Movie Rating System

Work & Prosperity	>	Loving Your Work
Relationships	>	Boss/Employee, Lovers
Transitions	>	Changing Careers
Overcoming Obstacles	>	Creative Expression, Entrapment

Guess Who

This film is the funny flip side of the original *Guess Who's Coming to Dinner*, proving that a father's consternation about his daughter's upcoming marriage is universal, and racial prejudice works both ways. Theresa (Saldana) brings her fiancé home to meet the family without mentioning that he's white. So father Percy (Mac) greets the black cabdriver with a welcoming handshake as Simon (Ashton) unloads the bags from the trunk. So begins the ever-so-slow thaw of the curmudgeon bank manager Percy to the idea that this white stockbroker, who has just quit his job, is going to join his family. The story turns into an awkward buddy film because Percy won't let Simon out of his sight, even sleeping with him in the basement, just to be sure. Forget the comparisons to the original film, these actors play off each others' screen personas perfectly. Mac's comedic posture as the gruff, skeptical, but somehow adorable grouch is a hilarious counterpoint to Kutcher's loveable goofball, who might just punk his future father-in-law when he's not looking.

DVD Release/Run Time	:	2005/105 minutes
Director	:	Kevin Rodney Sullivan
Cast	:	Bernie Mac, Ashton Kutcher, Zoe Saldana

Laugh & Cry Movie Rating System

Relationships	>	Fiancé
Finding Love	>	20s
Transitions	>	Getting Married
Overcoming Obstacles	>	Racial Prejudice

Harold and Maude

This wonderful cult favorite is a March-December romance between rich, despondent 20-year-old man/child Harold (Cort), who is obsessed with death, and a vivacious 79-year-old Maude (Gordon), who meet at a stranger's funeral. While Harold is faking suicides in front of his mother and the girls she fixes him up with, Maude shows him a whole new perspective about how to embrace life for all its delights. Just before her 80th birthday, Harold proposes marriage to Maude, but Maude hasn't finished her lessons for Harold. She has an inspired surprise that leaves you feeling happy and uplifted at the end of the movie, and that may linger for days after. Ranked #4 in Entertainment Weekly's Top 50 Cult Movies, it's one of those films that is a joy to watch and savor every time.

DVD Release/Run Time	:	1971/91 minutes
Director	:	Hal Ashby
Cast	:	Bud Cort, Ruth Gordon

Laugh & Cry Movie Rating System

Relationships	>	Lovers
Finding Love	>	Radical Age Differences
Overcoming Obstacles	>	Age Prejudice

High Fidelity

The comic-tragic story of painfully postponed male relationship maturity is familiar, but the 90s dance club mood and the Chicago neighborhood rock-record-store vibe set this one apart. Commitment-phobic 30s man-child Rob Gordon (Cusack) looks up five old girlfriends to find out what went wrong after his most recent live-in lawyer love Laura (superb Danish actress Hjelje) moves out abruptly and moves in with a neighbor (Robbins). Once a popular club DJ, Rob now makes a marginal living with his record store, where he indulges in his obsession of making Top 5 song lists and bantering about obscure cuts with his two clerks (Black, Louiso), who continue to show up, even though he no longer pays them. Rob starts his old-lovers quest with his first crush from junior high and works through several high school affairs and his college crush, Charlie (Zeta-Jones). Everything comes into focus when Laura's father dies and she invites him to the funeral. Don't miss Black's spot on cover of Marvin Gaye's "Let's Get It On" in the heartwarming close-out club scene.

DVD Release/Run Time	:	2000/113 minutes
Director	:	Stephen Frears
Cast	:	John Cusack, Iben Hjelje, Jack Black, Lisa Bonet, Catherine Zeta-Jones, Tim Robbins

Laugh & Cry Movie Rating System

Relationships	>	Lovers
Finding Love	>	30s
Transitions	>	Moving Out/Separating

Hitch

The always affable Will Smith does the near impossible with this film – he delivers a guys' romantic comedy that guys can actually love. Smith plays Alex "Hitch" Hitchens, a successful, under-the-radar NYC dating coach who, natch, has commitment issues of his own. Take Hitch's client Albert Brennaman (James), a klutzy accountant with a seemingly impossible crush on his glitzy celebrity client Allegra Cole (Valletta). The coaching lessons between the two are amusing and adorable, a 21st century Laurel and Hardy on a date riff. Hitch is surprised and intrigued when he falls for cool, crusty, workaholic gossip columnist Sara Melas (Mendes), who starts to thaw, but refreezes her frosty demeanor despite Hitch's best tricks. She goes into her investigative reporter mode and "outs" Hitch, which blows up his business. A great, fun date movie that dudes can't complain about and chicks can enjoy.

DVD Release/Run Time	:	2005/118 minutes
Director	:	Andy Tennant
Cast	:	Will Smith, Kevin James, Eva Mendes, Amber Valletta

Laugh & Cry Movie Rating System

Work & Prosperity	>	Loving Your Work
Relationships	>	Lovers
Finding Love	>	30s
Transitions	>	Courting

Holiday

This classic George Cukor screwball comedy is about a rich family where the black sheep sister Linda Seton (Hepburn) steals her sister Julia's fiancé, in one of the best Hepburn-Grant films. When successful businessman Johnny Case (Grant) becomes engaged to conformist Julia, she looks forward to Johnny joining her father's bank and continuing her wealthy lifestyle. Johnny, on the other hand, has more unconventional plans and would rather retire young, explore the world, and enjoy life as a holiday. This idea throws Julia into a panic. The rebellious Linda lends a sympathetic ear and understanding heart to Johnny's aspirations. The comical "change partners and dance" begins, as Johnny begins to realizes that he may be with the wrong sister.

DVD Release/Run Time	:	1938/93 minutes
Director	:	George Cukor
Cast	:	Cary Grant, Katharine Hepburn

Laugh & Cry Movie Rating System

Work & Prosperity	>	Realizing Dreams
Relationships	>	Lovers, Siblings
Finding Love	>	30s
Transitions	>	Changing Careers
Overcoming Obstacles	>	Class Prejudice, Entrapment

The Holiday

Here's a Christmas confection conjured up with incredibly beautiful actors and picture-perfect locations in a gated LA home and English stone cottage by romantic comedy master Nancy Meyers. Two women traumatized by broken love affairs decide on the spur of the moment to swap houses over the holiday. Amanda (Diaz), a successful movie trailer company owner, had her live-in film composer boyfriend move out abruptly. She looks forward to solitary holiday time licking her wounds in snowy Britain. Iris (Winslet), a downtrodden book editor, has been in a three year on-again, off-again relationship with a cad of a colleague (Sewell), who recently became engaged to a woman in Circulation, but still wants to continue dating her. Both meet-cute with men in their swapped homes – Iris has to figure out the high tech gate to let movie composer (Black) in to pick up some things for Amanda's ex. Amanda is wakened by Iris' brother Graham (Law), who arrives tipsy and in need of a place to crash after a late night at the pub. Of course, we can guess how it's all going to turn out, but it's a great big beautiful ride times two. This is one of those Christmas DVDs you'll want to watch to lift your holiday spirits in the season.

DVD Release/Run Time	:	2006/138 minutes
Director	:	Nancy Meyers
Cast	:	Cameron Diaz, Jude Law, Kate Winslet, Jack Black, Rufus Sewell

Laugh & Cry Movie Rating System

Relationships	>	Lovers
Finding Love	>	30's
Transitions	>	Courting
Overcoming Obstacles	>	Entrapment

How to Lose a Guy In 10 Days

Never underestimate the power of a wager to keep a guy's attention in a challenging new relationship. Hip women's magazine columnist Andie (Hudson) dreams of being a serious investigative reporter when her boss assigns her an article about how to lose a guy in 10 days, due in 11 days. A couple of women from an ad agency overhear the conversation. Later that evening in a yuppie watering hole, they bet their office "ladies man" Ben (McConaughey) that he can't seduce Andie in 10 days. The ad ladies want to beat out Ben for a shot at managing a new jewelry account. Andie proceeds to make every major mistake with Ben that a girl can make in a budding relationship. She's needy. She cries. She whines. She moves pink girly stuff into his apartment. As her article deadline is fast approaching, Andie cannot believe that Ben is still sticking around for more. This film is a fun fantasy with a few new twists on the old boy meets girl story. Now class, all you have to do is sit back and enjoy this very funny lesson.

DVD Release/Run Time	:	2003/116 minutes
Director	:	Donald Petrie
Cast	:	Kate Hudson, Mathew McConaughey

Laugh & Cry Movie Rating System

Relationships	>	Lovers
Finding Love	>	30s
Transitions	>	Courting

I Was a Male War Bride

The title says it all in this classic Howard Hawks screwball comedy where the sexual roles are reversed to hilarious effect. French captain Henri Rouchard (Grant) first hates and then falls in love with American Lt. Catherine Gates (Sheridan) while they are assigned to work together in Germany at the end of World War II. When Catherine's unit is recalled to the US, the only way to stay together is to marry under the US War Bride's Act. The couple proceeds to get tangled up in a series of amusing military mishaps. All the paperwork and billeting assignments presume the emigrating spouse is a woman. The wacky fun escalates as the captain can barely contain his exasperation after each incident. His wife's nonchalance about each frustrating event only heightens her husband's irritation. Don't miss one of the great, and underrated, Grant comedic performances in perfect partnership with Ann Sheridan.

DVD Release/Run Time	:	1949/105 minutes
Director	:	Howard Hawks
Cast	:	Cary Grant, Ann Sheridan

Laugh & Cry Movie Rating System

Relationships	>	Married Couples
Finding Love	>	30s
Transitions	>	Marrying

Impromptu

Set in 1830s France, this is a riotous romantic comedy based on the true stories of the cross-dressing, radical feminist novelist George Sand (Davis) and her ambitious artistic friends, lovers, and ex-lovers. Her circle of acquaintances included the French painter Delacroix, the Hungarian pianist Liszt (Sands), the Polish composer Chopin (Grant), and the French poet de Musset (Patinkin), as they all spend a fortnight in the French country as guests of the nervous, artistically aspirational Duchess D'Antan (Thompson). The group practices their respective crafts, perform, quarrel, duel, and act like temperamental artists. As Sand bickers with ex-lovers and falls for the sickly Chopin, the group barely conceals its disdain for their overeager, social-climbing hostess. Who knew a historical costume picture could be this laugh-out-loud funny?

DVD Release/Run Time	:	1991/107 minutes
Director	:	James Lapine
Cast	:	Judy Davis, Hugh Grant, Mandy Patinkin, Bernadette Peters, Julian Sands, Emma Thompson

Laugh & Cry Movie Rating System

Work & Prosperity	>	Loving Your Work
Relationships	>	Lovers
Finding Love	>	30s
Overcoming Obstacles	>	Creative Expression

In the Good Old Summertime

Here is *The Shop Around the Corner* story by the same writer, Miklos Laszlo, remade into a MGM musical with Judy Garland and Van Johnson. Two shop clerks, Veronica and Andrew, strike up a relationship as pen pals in search of true love. When they meet as clerks working in the same music store, they cannot stand each other. Andrew finds out who Veronica really is, but keeps it a secret between the musical numbers. Then it's Andrew's turn to figure out how to let Veronica in on the secret. Memorable songs include *I Don't Care*. Buster Keaton conceived and directed some comic sequences for Van Johnson. Despite the title, most of the movie takes place in the winter. This is Liza Minelli's first movie as the toddler of her mother Judy Garland's character at the end of the movie. The same story was remade with an electronic twist as *You've Got Mail* with Tom Hanks and Meg Ryan.

DVD Release/Run Time	:	1949/102 minutes
Director	:	Robert Z. Leonard
Cast	:	Judy Garland, Van Johnson, Buster Keaton

Laugh & Cry Movie Rating System

Relationships	>	Lovers
Finding Love	>	20s

Irreconcilable Differences

This Charles Shyer-Nancy Meyers film provides an amusing look at the tradeoffs ambitious parents make between their careers and their children. Adorable nine-year-old Casey (Barrymore) sues her squabbling parents (O'Neal and Long) for a divorce, so she can live in peace with her lovingly attentive Hispanic nanny. Her parents' seesawing careers are always out of sync. First, her father Albert Brodsky becomes a successful film director, after co-writing his first screenplay, while her mother Lucy stays home. Then, her father falls for starlet Blake (Stone), neglects Casey, and divorces Lucy. His next film with Blake bombs and his career skids to a halt. Only then does Albert start paying attention to Casey again. Meanwhile, Lucy pours all her frustrations as a scorned woman into a potboiler novel that becomes a best seller. As her career becomes demanding, it is Lucy's turn to neglect Casey. Their daughter's divorce action starts to level out the emotional teeter totter in the Brodsky family, with Casey controlling the balance. Not bad for a nine-year-old who acts more adult than her parents!

DVD Release/Run Time	:	1984/112 minutes
Director	:	Charles Shyer
Cast	:	Ryan O'Neal, Shelley Long, Drew Barrymore, Sam Wanamaker, Sharon Stone

Laugh & Cry Movie Rating System

Work & Prosperity	>	Balancing Work & Family
Relationships	>	Parent/Child, Two-Career Couples
Finding Love	>	20s, 30s
Transitions	>	Changing Careers, Divorcing
Overcoming Obstacles	>	Loss

It Happened One Night

With genuine 1930s atmosphere, every scene in this classic romantic comedy remains as fresh and funny today as when it was created. Rebellious socialite Ellie Andrews (Colbert) is on the run from her family and a cynical unemployed reporter Peter Warne (Gable), looking for a good story, helps her get from Florida back to New York. The groundbreaking film established the screwball comedy form that has been used ever since. The Production Code, passed in 1934, censored sexual content, challenging the writers to come up with less explicit, more hilarious ways around it. For example, the Walls of Jericho blanket is placed between the two twin beds in the motel room where Ellie and Peter spend one night, while Peter describes how a man undresses with lots of innuendo. Very funny and very sexy at the same time. Take that, you censors. When Peter shows up on Ellie's wedding day to claim his expenses for the trip and doesn't ask for the reward money, her father starts to understand that Peter might be a good match for his headstrong daughter.

DVD Release/Run Time	:	1934/105 minutes
Director	:	Frank Capra
Cast	:	Clark Gable, Claudette Colbert

Laugh & Cry Movie Rating System

Relationships	>	Parent/Child, Lovers
Finding Love	>	20s
Transitions	>	Marrying, Separating
Overcoming Obstacles	>	Class Prejudice, Entrapment

Knight's Tale, A

Before he was the Joker in *The Dark Knight*, Heath Ledger was pretending to be a knight in the riotous medieval farce about a young English squire on a quest to change his stars. When his knight dies, he creates a new identity with the help of the poet Chaucer (Bettany), who writes fake royal papers, his two fellow squires (Addy, Tudyk), who help him practice for tournaments, and a lady blacksmith who repairs his armor. He enters a jousting tournament and wins to the beat of the rock anthem *We Will Rock You*. He continues a winning streak in other tournaments with equally driving, ironic rock tunes like War's *Low Rider* and Sly and the Family Stone's *Gonna Take You Higher*. Along the way, he falls for a princess and meets an English prince. Don't miss this great bit of merriment from Oscar-winning writer-director Brian Helgeland (*L.A. Confidential, Mystic River*).

DVD Release/Run Time	:	2001/132 minutes
Director	:	Brian Helgeland
Cast	:	Heath Ledger, Mark Addy, Paul Bettany,
		Alan Tudyk, Rufus Sewell

Laugh & Cry Movie Rating System

Work & Prosperity	>	Realizing Dreams
Transitions	>	Changing Careers
Relationships	>	Friends
Finding Love	>	20s
Overcoming Obstacles	>	Class Prejudice

L.A. Story

This is writer-actor Steve Martin's delightfully quirky tale of romantic comedy set in his L.A. hometown. Shakespeare-spouting TV weatherman Harris K. Telemacher (Martin) receives a relationship epiphany from a billboard that tells him his life will change in two ways. He puts this revelation to immediate use as he attempts to win over a frosty English journalist, Sara McDowell (Tennant). The film is loaded with hilarious only-in-L.A. bits, like Harris driving three houses away from his to visit his neighbors, or being held up in an ATM line by a man who says, "Hi! I'm Bob and I'll be your robber tonight." Sarah Jessica Parker is delightful in her breakout film performance as Harris' bouncy young default date for an awkward weekend in Santa Barbara with two other couples, including Sara. Whether you love or hate L.A., this story leaves you laughing if you love it and crying if you don't.

DVD Release/Run Time	:	1991/95 minutes
Director	:	Mick Jackson
Cast	:	Steve Martin, Victoria Tennant, Richard E. Grant,
		Marilu Henner, Sarah Jessica Parker

Laugh & Cry Movie Rating System

Relationships	>	Lovers
Finding Love	>	30s
Transitions	>	Courting, Losing Mate

Lonely Hearts

This Australian film of midlife romance is a sweet, bemused slap-stick *Marty*, not a glamorous fantasy with gorgeous actors accessible only in your dreams, like *Nights in Rodanthe*. Never condescending, it is a funny, touching, honest story of real middle-aged singles working up the courage to reach through low self-esteem and loneliness and join the dating game in hopes of meeting an understanding mate. Folically-challenged Peter, constantly having mishaps with his ill-fitting toupee, signs up for a dating service and leaps into his journey to emotional evolution. Mousy Patricia (Hughes), in her 30s, still lives at home with mum. How each breaks through years of wounded isolation to find and accept each other is what makes this movie fun and unique. Winner of the Australian Film Institute Best Picture award, both lead actors and director were nominated as well.

DVD Release/Run Time	:	1982/106 minutes
Director	:	Paul Cox
Cast	:	Wendy Hughes, Norman Kaye

Laugh & Cry Movie Rating System

Relationships	>	Lovers
Finding Love	>	30s
Transitions	>	Courting

Love Actually

Love is in the air for nine couples in bitter and sweet stages of falling in and out of love in London in the five weeks before Christmas. Fading rocker Billy Mack (Nighy) starts rising in the charts once again. There's a newlywed couple (Knightley, Elijofor), where the bride realizes her husband's best friend is in love with her. The bachelor Prime Minister David (Grant) has feelings for his new catering manager Natalie (McCutcheon). His sister Karen (Thompson) is devastated to learn about her publisher husband Harry's (Rickman) flirtation with his editor Mia. Harry's top editor Sarah (Linney), with an institutionalized mentally ill brother, has a crush on art director Karl. Karen's friend Daniel (Neeson), recently widowed, discovers his 12-year-old stepson has a crush on a young American singer. Jamie (Firth), a writer jilted for his younger brother, goes to France to finish his novel and becomes infatuated with his maid Aurelia, who speaks neither English or French. Slacker Colin (Marshall) flies to Milwaukee to improve his chances of getting shagged in America. Don't forget the two movie stand-ins who become close after a simulated sex scene. Amazingly, writer/director Richard Curtis (*Four Weddings & A Funeral*) manages to get this diverse cast all to Heathrow for a rousing, feel-good holiday ending.

DVD Release/Run Time	:	2003/135 minutes
Director	:	Richard Curtis
Cast	:	Bill Nighy, Hugh Grant, Colin Firth, Emma Thompson, Alan Rickman, Liam Neeson, Keira Knightley, Chiwetel Eliojofor, Kris Marshall

Laugh & Cry Movie Rating System

Relationships	>	Lovers, Married Couples, Parent/Child
Finding Love	>	20s, 30s, 40s
Transitions	>	Marrying

Love Affair 1939

Told four times on film for each generation since 1932, this enchanting fantasy is guaranteed to get your tear ducts flowing and capture your heart. Writer/director Leo McCarey's 1939 remake stars Charles Boyer as a French playboy Michel Marnet and Irene Dunne as singer Terry McKay. It's a shipboard romance story between two people being "kept" by their respective fiancés. When Michel takes Kay to visit his grandmother (Ouspenskaya), you can sense Michel's feelings shifting from flirtation into love. The couple agrees to meet in six months at the top of the Empire State Building while each figures out how to become economically independent. On the way to the meeting, Terry has a tragic accident that leaves her unable to walk. She refuses to tell Michel. He tracks her down in her NY apartment at Chrismas in the marvelous three hanky final scene to be remembered for all time. This is a more concise telling of the story, without the distracting musical scenes in the 1957 version called *An Affair to Remember* with Cary Grant and Deborah Kerr. Warren Beatty and wife Annette Benning remade it again in 1994 as *Love Affair*. Unfortunately, the story suffers because the social mores have shifted significantly in the two generations since 1939.

DVD Release/Run Time	:	1939/87 minutes
Director	:	Leo McCarey
Cast	:	Charles Boyer, Irene Dunne, Maria Ouspenskaya

Laugh & Cry Movie Rating System

Relationships	>	Lovers
Finding Love	>	30s

Love Affair 1994

Husband and wife team Warren Beatty and Annette Benning did the third remake of this classic romance for the 90s generation, but in this case, the third time didn't have the charm of its other two Leo McCarey directed predecessors – the Charles Boyer/Irene Dunne *Love Affair* (1939) and the Cary Grant/Deborah Kerr *An Affair to Remember* (1957). The basic story premise was kept in tact, with a bit of modernization. This time around, Mike Gambril (Beatty) is a retired football star traveling on the same flight to Sydney as Terry McKay (Benning) when the plane crashes on a small Pacific island. The couple ends up falling in love, taking a rescue boat to a larger island, although each is engaged to another. The couple agrees to meet in three months to see if they still feel the same way, but Terry doesn't make it. It's unfortunate that Mr. Beatty didn't update this storyline like he did with *Heaven Can Wait*, a remake of the 1941 *Here Comes Mr. Jordan*, since the romantic mores have changed dramatically since the 50s. The highlight of this film is Katherine Hepburn's 10-minute appearance as Mike's aunt, her last motion picture role. The low point is the lack of on-screen chemistry between the married stars – both amazing actors in their own right. It's a wonder how they've had four children together.

DVD Release/Run Time	:	1994/108minutes
Director	:	Glenn Gordon Caron
Cast	:	Warren Beatty, Annette Benning, Katherine Hepburn

Laugh & Cry Movie Rating System

Relationships	>	Lovers
Finding Love	>	30s

Making Mr. Right

A captivating, upbeat, romantic spin on the Frankenstein theme, this film tells the tale of a nerdy scientist Dr. Jeff Peters (Malkovich), who replicates himself as an almost-human look-alike android Ulysses to take a long space journey. A stylish advertising whiz Frankie (Magnuson) is hired to promote the android astronaut concept to the public, but first she has to teach Ulysses some social skills that surprisingly makes him more human. Her marketing savvy immediately puts her at loggerheads with the emotionally-repressed Dr. Peters. As the doctor starts becoming more robot-like, his android counterpart Ulysses amazingly begins to acquire all-too-human feelings and emotions. Things get complicated when Ulysses starts to fall for Trish, and Trish becomes curious about how human he can be. What's a real live girl suppose to do? Malkovich's dual-role transformations, from android to human as Ulysses, and from sort of human to really withdrawn as Dr. Peters, is funny and fascinating.

DVD Release/Run Time : 1987/95 minutes
Director : Susan Seidelman
Cast : John Malkovich, Ann Magnuson, Glenne Headly

Laugh & Cry Movie Rating System

Work & Prosperity	>	Loving Your Work
Relationships	>	Colleagues & Co-Workers, Lovers
Finding Love	>	30s
Overcoming Obstacles	>	Creative Expression

The Matchmaker

This amusing bit of blarney tells the tale of Marcy (Garofalo), a high powered political aide to Boston U.S. Senator McGlory, who is dispatched to Ireland to locate his Celtic relatives to boost the Irish votes in his bid for re-election. The trouble is the town Ballinagra is in the middle of their annual matchmaking festival. Two rival matchmakers single out Marcy, even though she's only interested in finding the McGlory family history fast, and getting back to the U.S. The town genealogist slows her down by taking days to come up with any information. Marcy and burned-out journalist-turned-bartender Sean (O'Hara) start a dance as the matchmakers work their magic. When the search for McGlorys stalls, the Senator himself shows up and bags Sean's ex-wife, whose politically awesome maiden name is Kennedy. This part is tailor-made for Garofalo, with her comedic timing, her nonchalance about her good looks, and her tough career girl demeanor hiding a soft heart, while daring a man who is her equal to unlock it. Beautiful Irish scenery enhances this romantic escape.

DVD Release/Run Time	:	1997/97 minutes
Director	:	Marc Joffe
Cast	:	Janeane Garofalo, David O'Hara, Saffron Burrows, Denis Leary

Laugh & Cry Movie Rating System

Work & Prosperity	>	Balancing Work & Family
Relationships	>	Lovers
Finding Love	>	30s
Transitions	>	Courting

Me Myself I

Here's a funny single female angle on the mid-life relationship crisis. The male solution is to look up old girlfriends for feedback, but we've seen that before (*High Fidelity, Broken Flowers, Something's Gotta Give*). This amusing Australian film takes a sad and lonely single 30-something journalist (Griffiths from *Muriel's Wedding, Six Feet Under, Brothers & Sisters*) who fantasizes about accepting the college marriage proposal she turned down. Through a freak auto accident, she is dropped into an alternate reality where she did marry the guy and now has three kids… and a whole new set of comical problems. Let's see. There's an unaffectionate, neglectful husband; the pesky neighbor who wants to continue their affair; a rebellious, punked 13-year-old daughter; and two younger boys, one still in need of potty training help. And then there is her lack of time to practice her writing craft amidst the family chaos. Maybe the grass isn't greener on the other side, but it sure is entertaining to take an upside-down peek.

DVD Release/Run Time	:	1999/104 minutes
Director	:	Pip Karmel
Cast	:	Rachel Griffiths

Laugh & Cry Movie Rating System

Relationships	>	Lovers
Finding Love	>	30s
Transitions	>	Courting

Mississippi Masala

This is a jam-packed story of a prosperous Asian-Indian lawyer and his family who lost everything when Idi Amin kicked out all non-blacks out of Uganda in 1972. Jay (Seth), his wife Kinnu (Tagore) and their young daughter Meena (Choudhury) relocate to Mississippi where Jay operates a run-down motel and Kinnu owns a liquor store. Fast forward twenty years, Jay is still longing for his African life that cannot be and the property he lost there. Then 26-year-old American-raised Meena, working as a maid at the family motel, falls in love with black businessman Demetrius (Washington), who operates a motel rug cleaning service. This is not the life her educated parents had in mind for her, although in the Indian community, Meena is considered too dark-skinned and poor to make a desirable wife. Demetrius' conservative family also condemns the relationship after Indian motel owners boycott his business. This is a funny, ironic commentary on racism and the definition of African, as seen through black and Indian eyes.

DVD Release/Run Time	:	1992/118 minutes
Director	:	Mira Nair
Cast	:	Denzel Washington, Sarita Choudhury, Roshan Seth, Charles S. Dutton, Sharmila Tagore

Laugh & Cry Movie Rating System

Work & Prosperity	>	Realizing Dream
Relationships	>	Parent/Child, Lovers
Finding Love	>	20s
Transitions	>	Moving Out/Separating
Overcoming Obstacles	>	Racial Prejudices, Cultural Abilities

A Month by the Lake

Set in 1937 Lake Como, Italy, in a seemingly peaceful pause before World War II, this is a charming romantic triangle comedy of manners. Miss Bentley (Redgrave) has been summering at the stunning Lake Como villa for 16 years with her London portrait painter father, who recently passed away. Stuck with obnoxious Americans, her interest is piqued when British Major Wilshaw (Fox) shows up and asks her out for a drink, although she inadvertently stands him up. When Miss Beaumont (Thurman) dabbles with the Major's affections, it revives feelings he hasn't felt since the Great War. It's fun to sit back, enjoy the spectacular scenery, and watch the older lovers finally break through their British reserve to express their true feelings. You're left to bask in the glow of their romantic hope. Redgrave received a Golden Globe nomination for her role.

DVD Release/Run Time	:	1995/91 minutes
Director	:	John Irvin
Cast	:	Vanessa Redgrave, Edward Fox, Uma Thurman

Laugh & Cry Movie Rating System

Relationships	>	Lovers
Finding Love	>	40s
Transitions	>	Courting
Overcoming Obstacles	>	Age Prejudice

Much Ado About Nothing

Who says Shakespeare can't be fun and fast-paced? An all-star cast romping through a beautiful villa in Italy gives rise to a bawdy telling of the Bard's tale of courting and deception. Claudio (Leonard) and Hero (Beckinsale), a young couple filled with the innocent dew of love's first touch, are to be married in a week. They decide that before their wedding, they will trick confirmed bachelor Benedick (Branagh) and Beatrice (Thompson), the jaded 30-something couple who constantly bicker in sarcastic rhyme, into declaring love for each other. In the meantime, the evil Don John (Reeves) conspires to break up the happy young couple by accusing Hero of infidelity. With more plot twists than Italian spiralini pasta, it all turns out to be much ado about nothing, with lots of laughs along the way.

VD Release/Run Time	:	1993/111
Director	:	Kenneth Branagh
Cast	:	Kenneth Branagh, Denzel Washington, Michael Keaton, Emma Thompson, Robert Sean Leonard, Kate Beckinsale, Keanu Reeves

Laugh & Cry Movie Rating System

Relationships	>	Lovers
Finding Love	>	30s, Teen Years
Transitions	>	Courting, Marrying

Muriel's Wedding

An overweight young woman (Collette) from the backwater town of Porpoise Spit, Queensland with a hopelessly comical dysfunctional family, lifts herself out of her boring life in the sticks with ABBA songs and fantasies about her picture-perfect wedding. In fact, when she relocates to Sydney with her friend (Griffiths), she compulsively tries on wedding dresses, relating her dreams / lies to the gullible bridal sales clerks without a thought about a possible groom. All at once, her wishes start coming true when a rich, handsome South African Olympic swimmer offers to pay her to marry him so he can become a citizen and qualify for the Australian swim team. Infused with cheery ABBA tunes, this movie captures just the right balance of young 20s optimism and the complicated hand life deals someone who doesn't exactly fit. No matter how many times you watch it, it still feels fresh and uplifting with lots of chuckles.

DVD Release/Run Time	:	1995/106 minutes
Director	:	P J Hogan
Cast	:	Toni Collette, Rachel Griffiths

Laugh & Cry Movie Rating System

Relationships	>	Lovers
Finding Love	>	20s
Transitions	>	Courting

Murphy's Romance

Feisty divorced mom Emma Moriarty (Fields) moves to a dusty, small Texas town and pours all her energy into making a go of a horse ranch. There she meets an eccentric widowed pharmacist, Murphy Jones (Garner), with a beloved antique car he still drives to work, a horse to board, and a job for her young teen son, Jake (Heim). Out of the blue, her man/child ex-husband Bobby Jack (Kerwin) shows up, expecting a place to freeload and trying to sweet talk Emma into getting back together for Jake's sake. Reluctantly, she puts Bobby Jack to work as a ranch hand and starts inviting Murphy to supper for some adult conversation. So the romantic two-step kicks off for the threesome. Garner and Fields' on-screen sizzle resulted in Oscar and Golden Globe nominations. The striking cinematography captures the spare small town beauty and received an Oscar nod as well. Here's a happy, heartwarming trail ride from "Stay to supper, Murphy?" to "How do you like your eggs in the morning?" that you may want to hop on more than once.

DVD Release/Run Time	:	1986/107 minutes
Director	:	Martin Ritt

Cast: Sally Fields, James Garner, Corey Heim, Brian Kerwin

Laugh & Cry Movie Rating System

Relationships	>	Lovers
Finding Love	>	Radical Age Difference
Transitions	>	Courting

Music and Lyrics

A funny feel-good spin on the pop music business, now – ala a young pop diva – and then – ala a Wham-like duo – is whirled into an odd couple working relationship that mellows into a romantic partnership. The opening credits roll over with a sly 80s salute to MTV music videos where Alex Fletcher (Grant) is part of the hugely successful duo called Pop. Fast forward to 21st century NYC, he is now lucky to have gigs at state fairs, amusement parks, and high school reunions. Out of the blue, he gets a call from the hottest pop star of the moment, Cora (Bennett), who was a big fan of Pop when she was seven. Cora gives him a shot at writing a new song for her called *A Way Back into Love* in just five days. Problem is, Alex only writes music, not lyrics. Enter aspiring writer Sophie (Barrymore), who is watering his plants for a friend. She uses her poetic ear to finish lyrics that stump a professional lyricist Alex is working with. This starts the crash project that's a lot like a finals week study jam. The warmhearted story wraps up at the Cora concert. Be sure to watch the final credits with hilarious pop-up balloon commentary about what happens to everyone afterwards. You may just end up humming some of those bouncy old school tunes.

DVD Release/Run Time	:	2007/96 minutes
Director	:	Marc Lawrence
Cast	:	Drew Barrymore, Hugh Grant, Brad Garrett, Kristen Johnston, Haley Bennett

Laugh & Cry Movie Rating System

Work & Prosperity	>	Realizing Dreams
Relationships	>	Lovers
Finding Love	>	30s
Transitions	>	Courting
Overcoming Obstacles	>	Loss, Creative Expression

My Best Friend's Wedding

When Julianne's (Roberts) college best friend Michael (Mulroney) announces that he's engaged, she suddenly realizes that she's been in love with him all along. Her terror of expressing her true feelings propels her into funny, frantic last-minute action to try to stop the wedding. It's a loopy look at a desperate woman doing desperate things, creating comic chaos in her wake. Julianne is forced to reassess her motives when she meets Michael's fiancé Kimberly (Diaz), who is surprisingly sweet. The hilarious movie shows how Julianne goes through major attitude adjustments to get herself lined up with the realities of the wedding, including a very funny group sing of *I Say a Little Prayer for You*. For support, she invites her gay friend (Everett) to front as her fiancé in a series of amusingly awkward moments. Here's a recipe for anyone with unrequited love regrets: 1) Watch this movie. 2) Hum *What the World Needs Now* when you're feeling doubts. Repeat the first two steps until you're ready to move on.

DVD Release/Run Time	:	1997/105 minutes
Director	:	P J Hogan
Cast	:	Julia Roberts, Dermot Mulroney, Cameron Diaz, Rupert Everett

Laugh & Cry Movie Rating System

Relationships	>	Friends
Finding Love	>	30s
Transitions	>	Marrying

My Big Fat Greek Wedding

With a wonderful, warm-hearted script by Greek-American actress/writer Nina Vardalos, this movie takes an affectionate look at how a 30s ugly duckling working in the family restaurant is turned into a travel agent swan through a romance with an upper class American (Corbett) who asks to marry her. She has to deal with all the recent immigrant inadvertent hilarity, like her father's contention that all words come originally from Greek roots, blithely providing convoluted explanations for any word, even kimono. Of course, there are lots of laughs when her whole Greek family shows up to meet the future WASP in-laws, who are stuffy, confused, and overwhelmed by her family's Mediterranean customs, setting the stage for the wedding finale. This is a film that manages to be funny, sweet, and loveable every time you watch it.

DVD Release/Run Time	:	2002/95 minutes
Director	:	Joel Zwick
Cast	:	Nina Vardalos, John Corbett, Lainie Kazan,
		Michael Constantine

Laugh & Cry Movie Rating System

Relationships	>	Lovers
Finding Love	>	30s
Transitions	>	Courting
Overcoming Obstacles	>	Class Prejudice

Mystic Pizza

A sweetly-told and often side-splitting story is about three Portuguese-American high school friends who work at the local pizza restaurant in Mystic, CT, waiting out that time between high school graduation and the next stage of their lives. It contrasts the working class experience slinging pizza and cleaning fish with the upper crust country club diners feasting on lobster in this quaint tourist town. The film kicks off with a comical wedding altar scene. Jojo (Taylor) can't decide whether to marry the local fisherman Bill (D'Onofrio) she's crazy about because she fears she'll be re-creating her parents' life. Ambitious, brainy Kat (Gish) is saving money to go to Yale by working three jobs. She is enticed into an affair with the architect father (Moses) of her babysitting charge. Her sexy, aimless "bad" sister Daisy (Roberts) starts dating a preppy law school dropout and doesn't have any particular plans about what's next for her. This film was Julia Robert's breakout role that led to her being cast in her Oscar-winning role in *Steel Magnolias*.

DVD Release/Run Time	:	1988/101 minutes
Director	:	Daniel Petrie
Cast	:	Annabeth Gish, Julia Roberts, Lili Taylor,
		Vincent D'Onofrio, William R. Moses

Laugh & Cry Movie Rating System

Work & Prosperity	>	Realizing Dream
Relationships	>	Friends, Lovers
Finding Love	>	College Years
Transitions	>	Moving Out/Separating
Overcoming Obstacles	>	Class Prejudice, Entrapment

Next Stop Wonderland

Listen to a sexy Jobim samba on a wintry Boston beach near Wonderland, where two strangers meet by chance, and you have the contrasting moods of this indie romance about an underachieving night nurse Erinne (Davis), whose overachieving mother (Holland) places a personal ad for her daughter that's a better description of the older woman than the younger. Lots of awkward and amusing first dates ensue, as Erinne reluctantly sifts through 63 phone messages from men who want to meet a woman who fits the ad's description. In a parallel story, a plumber is studying to be a marine biologist, while paying off his father's gambling debts to a mobster at the Wonderland dog track. His lawyer brother and a couple of friends make a bet about the results of answering Erinne's ad. This film offers a fresh, funny snapshot of a woman in her 30s, dumped by her boyfriend, on the emotional arc from enjoying being alone now, to being ill-at-ease with personal ad dating, to warming to the possibility of a relationship – as gentle, relaxed, and easy as a Brazilian dance.

DVD Release/Run Time	:	1998/104 minutes
Director	:	Brad Anderson
Cast	:	Hope Davis, Taylor Holland, Phillip Seymour Hoffman

Laugh & Cry Movie Rating System

Relationships	>	Lovers
Finding Love	>	30s
Transitions	>	Courting
Overcoming Obstacles	>	Loss

Notting Hill

Here's another fun romantic fantasy from prolific comedy scribe Richard Curtis (*Four Weddings & A Funeral*, *Love Actually*, *Bridget Jones 1 & 2*) about a famous American actress, Anna Scott (Roberts), who falls for an unassuming, hapless Notting Hill bookseller, William Thacker (Grant). They meet-cute when Anna comes into William's bookshop, flustering him and his clerk. Incredulous about meeting her, William bumps into her again. This time he inadvertently spills juice all over her. Anna returns to his apartment for a change of clothes and a light kiss that leads to something more. The amusement escalates as modest William is uncomfortably forced to juggle turn-coat friends, including wacky flatmate Spike (in an inspired go-for-it performance by Ifans), and the hounding press hoards just to spend a bit of time with Anna. Nominated for three Golden Globe awards (Best Picture, Best Actor, and Best Actress), this movie offers up the hope that the rest of us can join the stars, at least for a couple of hours.

DVD Release/Run Time	:	1999/124 minutes
Director	:	Roger Michell
Cast	:	Julia Roberts, Hugh Grant, Rhys Ifans

Laugh & Cry Movie Rating System

Relationships	>	Lovers
Finding Love	>	30s
Overcoming Obstacles	>	Class Obstacles

Peter's Friends

This underrated British film unfortunately got lost with unfair comparisons to *Big Chill*. It is a witty, sarcastic, and intelligent account of an English university comedy troupe of six players, who scattered to London and L.A. and reunite ten years later for a New Year's weekend at Peter's (Fry) recently inherited British country manor. Each one has their problems. Andrew (Branagh) went to Hollywood, married sitcom star Carol (Rudner) and now writes for her, but their relationship is strained. Sarah (Emmanuel), who still falls for unavailable men, brings a not-yet-divorced man to the party. Roger (Laurie) and Mary (Staunton) married each other and have a very successful music jingle business, but are emotionally frozen by the loss of their child. With her biological clock in alarm mode and still seeking "Mr. Right," Maggie (Thompson) thinks Peter might just be the man for her, but Peter harbors a secret that will make that difficult.

DVD Release/Run Time	:	1992/100 minutes
Director	:	Kenneth Branagh
Cast	:	Emma Thompson, Kenneth Branagh, Rita Rudner,
		Hugh Laurie, Imelda Staunton, Stephen Fry,
		Alphonsia Emmanuel

Laugh & Cry Movie Rating System

Work & Prosperity	>	Realizing Dreams
Relationships	>	Friends, Married Couples
Finding Love	>	30s
Transitions	>	Midlife Crisis
Overcoming Obstacles	>	Creative Expression, Loss

The Philadelphia Story

Classic romantic comedy doesn't get any better than this amusing fable of a spoiled rich girl, Tracy Lord (Hepburn), who is about to marry an eager social climber when her first husband C. K. Dexter Haven (Grant) appears to muck up the pre-nuptial preparations. Added to the comical confusion is a reporter (Stewart) and photographer (Hussey) from a scandal magazine, who is holding Tracy hostage for her nuptial news, in exchange for suppressing her estranged father's amorous indiscretions. As Tracy and her family try to keep a stiff upper class lip about the out-of-control events, the news team is busy sniffing out even more gossip with the jaded eye of working class folks. The day before the wedding, Tracy has her doubts and falls into a boozy night of questioning her fate with the reporter. We can guess the outcome, but it's a rollicking good ride with an outstanding cast. Jimmy Stewart won his only Oscar for Best Actor and Donald Ogden Stewart won for Best Screenplay.

DVD Release/Run Time	:	1940/112 minutes
Director	:	George Cukor
Cast	:	Katherine Hepburn, Cary Grant, Jimmy Stewart, Ruth Hussey

Laugh & Cry Movie Rating System

Relationships	>	Married Couples
Finding Love	>	30s
Transitions		Marrying

Pillow Talk

No romantic comedy guide is complete without at least one 1950s Rock Hudson-Doris Day movie. In *Pillow Talk*, composer and ladies' man Brad Allen (Hudson) shares a New York City back-in-the-day party telephone line with decorator Jan Morrow (Day). They loathe each other, although they've never met. When they do, Brad realizes who she is and fakes an obvious Texas name "Rex Stetson" and accent as a way to get to know her better. Triple divorced Jonathon (Randall), Brad's producer and friend, has his sites set on Jan as wife #4, without really asking her to marry him. The delightful confusion compounds until Jan learns the truth about Brad/Rex. Doris' pre-feminist banter along with her wardrobe are still sharp today. Her close-ups through Vaseline-smeared lens are a bit much today, but her on-screen chemistry with Rock is just right. Despite what we now know about Rock, there's no denying the 34-year-old hunk can still trigger delicious fantasies for both girls—and boys.

DVD Release/Run Time	:	1959/102 minutes
Director	:	Michael Gordon
Cast	:	Doris Day, Rock Hudson, Tony Randall

Laugh & Cry Movie Rating System

Relationships	>	Lovers
Finding Love	>	30s
Transitions	>	Courting

Pretty Woman

This classic "hooker with a heart of gold" fantasy is elevated by Julia Roberts' Oscar-nominated go-for-it performance as Vivian Ward, and Richard Gere's turn as the conflicted, cold-hearted business mogul Edward Lewis, who needs an escort for a week of tricky, complicated business negotiations. Edward finances Vivian's transformation from trashy streetwalker to elegant escort with a carte blanche makeover and shopping spree on Rodeo Drive. She takes etiquette lessons from the knowing, but discreet hotel manager (Elizondro). Vivian turns out to be a convincing quick study among Edward's business colleagues and the gold diggers out to snare his checkbook. During their time together, Vivian begins to understand how to thaw Edward's heart and coax out the wounded man/child who has a paralyzing fear of heights. Despite the R-rating, director Marshall injects large doses of funny, feel-good action with a sure-to-please, happy ending.

DVD Release/Run Time	:	1990/119 minutes
Director	:	Garry Marshall
Cast	:	Richard Gere, Julia Roberts,
		Hector Elizondro, Jason Alexander

Laugh & Cry Movie Rating System

Relationships > Lovers

Finding Love > 20s, 40s

Transitions > Courting

Overcoming Obstacles > Class Prejudice

Pride and Prejudice (1995)

You've got to hand it to Jane Austen, a shy English spinster with a wonderful wit and timeless imagination who died a virgin at 41, for writing the novel *Pride and Prejudice* in her early 20s, thus inventing the first romantic comedy and the definitive template for all subsequent romantic farce. For Colin Firth lovers, this lavish five hour mini-series has unequaled charm. The classic tale of a genteel English family anxiously attempting to marry off five daughters with no dowry remains as fresh and funny today as when it was first written in 1797. Independent Elizabeth Bennett (Ehle) is reluctantly smitten with the arrogant, wealthy Mr. Darcy (Firth), while her sister Jane (Harker) falls for Darcy's best friend Mr. Bingley (Bonham-Carter). Both older sisters try to cope with their silly, ill-mannered mother (a delightful Steadman) and their three younger sisters, who shamelessly pursue local soldiers. The youngest, Lydia, jeopardizes all the Bennett girls' chance for matrimony by running off with the handsome scoundrel Mr. Wickham, son of Mr. Darcy's father's estate manager. A rousing piano score punctuates the angst and absurdity against a period-perfect backdrop of Georgian England costumes and countryside scenery.

DVD Release/Run Time	:	1995/300 minutes
Director	:	Simon Langton
Cast	:	Jennifer Ehle, Colin Firth, Susannah Harker, Alison Steadman, Crispin Bonham-Carter

Laugh & Cry Movie Rating System

Relationships	>	Lovers
Finding Love	>	20s
Transitions	>	Courting

Pride and Prejudice (2005)

This 21st century retelling of Jane Austen's classic romantic comedy offers the first age-appropriate Elizabeth Bennett (the splendid Knightley at age 23). It's a grittier 1797 reality show of everyday detail with livestock running through the shabby Bennett manor, a slower early 19th century pacing, long lingering shots of the countryside, and authentic period music more like Schubert lullabies than an upbeat English Morris dance. Even Mr. Darcy (MacFayden) was purposely cast to be not too handsome, dashing many young viewers' fantasies. That said, it's a fresh take on the comic tale of a genteel family too poor to finance dowries for their five daughters because they have no male heir to retain the family estate. Mr. Bennett (Sutherland) is wonderfully warm-hearted, yet muddled about his family's plight, while Mrs. Bennett (Blethyn) is less hysterical and more sympathetic than in previous versions. Still, the two-hour condensation of the novel required some heavy-handed editing. The villain, Mr. Wickham, is reduced to a caricature with little screen time. The silly, sappy American ending, omitted from the British version, probably has poor Jane Austen still rolling around in her grave.

DVD Release/Run Time	:	2005/127 minutes
Director	:	Joe Wright
Cast	:	Keira Knightley, Matthew MacFayden, Donald Sutherland, Brenda Blethyn, Rosamund Pike, Simon Wood

Laugh & Cry Movie Rating System

Relationships	>	Lovers
Finding Love	>	20s
Transitions	>	Courting

Romancing the Stone

Here's a fun romantic comedy-adventure romp that will please both the girls and the boys. Reclusive romance novel writer Joan Wilder (Turner) receives a map in the mail from her recently murdered brother-in-law. She must travel to Columbia to ransom her kidnapped sister with this map. When Joan arrives, the situation is far riskier than she could imagine. She hires Jack T. Colton (Douglas) to help her negotiate with the hoodlums. Her rescue adventure with Jack becomes a more dangerous, yet comical real-life version of one of her book plots. Joan loses more than her shyness along the way and starts living up to her Wilder name, encouraged by Jack's swashbuckling ways. In the end, you can picture that bodice-ripping book cover of Joan's next novel with a man who might just resemble Jack.

DVD Release/Run Time	:	1984/106 minutes
Director	:	Robert Zemenkis
Cast	:	Michael Douglas, Kathleen Turner, Danny DeVito

Laugh & Cry Movie Rating System

Relationships	>	Lovers
Finding Love	>	30s
Transitions	>	Courting

A Room With a View

Indecisive young Englishwoman Lucy Honeychurch (Bonham Carter) and her spinster chaperone and guardian Charlotte Bartlett (Smith) take refuge in Florence pension rooms to contemplate Lucy's marital options. In a reservation mix up, they were not assigned the rooms with views they had expected. The first evening, they meet Mr. Emerson (Elliott) and his son George (Sands) who offer to exchange their view rooms for Lucy and Charlotte's rooms. As Lucy falls under the charming George's spell, Charlotte keeps reminding her that the sensible choice for a husband is the socially correct twit Cecil Vyse (Day- Lewis). Lucy's heartfelt choice of George leads her to all sorts of deceptions, trying to please everyone but herself. Based on E. M. Forster's novel, set in the lush Tuscan landscape to passionate Puccini tunes, with impeccable Merchant- Ivory-Jhabvala production values, and a superb and gorgeous cast, it doesn't get any more romantic than this film with a view of Florence from the heart.

DVD Release/Run Time	:	1986/117 minutes
Director	:	James Ivory
Cast	:	Helena Bonham Carter, Julian Sands, |
		Denholm Elliott, Maggie Smith, Judi Dench

Laugh & Cry Movie Rating System

Work & Prosperity	>	Realizing Dreams
Relationships	>	Lovers
Finding Love	>	20s
Transitions	>	Marrying
Overcoming Obstacles	>	Entrapment, Class Prejudice

Sense and Sensibility

The second family of the rich Mr. Dashwood (Wilkinson) is left impoverished at his death by British inheritance laws, where the entire estate goes to the eldest son by his first wife. The mother and her three daughters are offered a cottage by Sir John Middleton, a distant relative of Mrs. Dashwood (Jones). The older sisters, sensible Elinor (Thompson) and passionate Marianne (Winslet), have little hope of successful marriages without a dowry. Ardent Marianne is attracted to the debonair Mr. Willoughby (Wise), while reserved Elinor is intrigued by Edward Ferrars (Grant), the well-off brother of the wife of her half-brother John. But neither suitor can consider either sister as a serious marital prospect. Up for the challenge, Mrs. Jennings, Sir John's mother-in-law, goes into matchmaking high gear. After obsessive Marianne spurns her attempt to pair her with the older, wealthy Colonel Brandon (Rickman), Mrs. Jennings takes the Dashwood girls to London for the season to improve their possibilities. The lovingly crafted script, based on the Jane Austen novel, brought Thompson an Oscar. The comedic balance between irony and warmth is maintained perfectly by Ang Lee's understanding direction.

DVD Release/Run Time	:	1995/135 minutes
Director	:	Ang Lee
Cast	:	Emma Thompson, Hugh Grant, Kate Winslet, Alan Rickman, Greg Wise, Gemma Jones

Laugh & Cry Movie Rating System

Relationships	>	Lovers/Siblings
Finding Love	>	20s
Transitions	>	Courting
Overcoming Obstacles	>	Entrapment, Class Prejudice

Shakespeare in Love

This Elizabethan farce takes an ingenious look into the story behind the development of one of the Western world's favorite love stories, originally called Romeo and Ethel, the Pirate's Daughter. Will Shakespeare (Fiennes) is struggling to write a comedy for anxious Globe Theatre impresario (Rush) and his stage manager (Wilkinson), while carrying on a secret affair with Lady Viola (Paltrow) who serves as his muse. Viola has a passion for acting, despite the fact that acting was forbidden to women. She cross-dresses as a boy to audition for the Romeo part, while hiding it from her fiancé Lord Wessex (Firth). A splendid film that won seven Oscars for Best Picture, Best Actress (Platrow), Best Supporting Actress (Dench for eight show stopping minutes of screen time as Queen Elizabeth), Best Costumes, Best Art Direction, Best Screenplay written for the Screen, and Best Music Score. Me thinks the Bard would be amused, as will you.

DVD Release/Run Time	:	1999/123 minutes
Director	:	John Madden
Cast	:	Gwyneth Paltrow, Joseph Fiennes, Judy Dench,
		Geoffrey Rush, Tom Wilkinson, Colin Firth

Laugh & Cry Movie Rating System

Relationships	>	Lovers
Finding Love	>	20s
Transitions	>	Marrying
Overcoming Obstacles	>	Creative Expression

She's the One

This is a funny look at how one Irish-American family passes down relationship patterns from one generation to the next without even realizing it. Self-satisfied chauvinist Mr. Fitzpatrick (Mahoney) spouts very bad marital advice to his two sons, as his own marriage disintegrates and his wife leaves him without his knowledge. Slacker, taxi-driving Mickey (Burns) is sorting out the confusion of his own impulsive marriage to one of his fares, an art student named Hope (Bahns), whom he knew for only 24 hours. A couple of years before, Mickey had caught his ex-fiancé Heather (Diaz) with another man and has been licking his wounds ever since. Now his brother Francis (McGlone), a rich, Wall Street player, is two-timing his sexually frustrated wife Renee (Aniston) with Heather. Mickey tries to warn him that Heather is a gold digging nymphomaniac, but Francis won't listen as he dumps Renee and asks Heather to marry him. For advice in figuring out if she's the one, in the Fitzpatrick family, father definitely does not know best.

DVD Release/Run Time	:	1996/95 minutes
Director	:	Edward Burns
Cast	:	Edward Burns, Mike McGlone, Jennifer Aniston,
		Cameron Diaz, Maxine Bahns, John Mahoney

Laugh & Cry Movie Rating System

Relationships	>	Multi-Generational Family, Married Couples
Finding Love	>	20s/50s
Transitions	>	Courting
Overcoming Obstacles	>	Entrapment

The Shop Around the Corner

Any compilation of romantic comedies must include the German master Ernst Lubitsch's most perfect romance. Two store clerks, Klara (Sullavan) and Alfred (Stewart), who work in a Budapest gift store can barely tolerate each other during the day, yet unbeknownst to the other, they pour their hearts out to each other in the evening in hopes of finding true love. Their daytime disdain for each other provides an amusing counterpoint to their evening ardor. The shop owner is about to fire Alfred because he mistakenly thinks he's having an affair with his wife, but when he learns otherwise, he promotes Alfred to manager. Meanwhile, Klara agrees to meet her penpal that evening at a café, holding a red carnation. When Alfred arrives, he sees her and decides to go in, but not reveal his identity to Klara, who is annoyed that he's even there. The next day when Klara finds out who her new boss is, she faints at the idea. Eventually, Alfred lets her in on his secret very gently. Such delicious storytelling! No wonder it was called the Lubitsch touch. The same story was used again in the 1949 Judy Garland MGM musical *In the Good Old Summertime* and inspired Nora Ephron's electronic age revision *You've Got Mail*.

DVD Release/Run Time	: 1940/99 minutes
Director	: Ernst Lubitsch
Cast	: Margaret Sullavan, Jimmy Stewart

Laugh & Cry Movie Rating System

Relationships	>	Lovers
Finding Love	>	20s
Transitions	>	Courting

Shrek

This very funny, fractured fairy tale for kids of all ages is about an ogre Shrek (Myers) whose swamp is overrun by all sorts of fairy tale characters, since the King kicked them out of his kingdom. The hilarious opening fairy tale sequence pokes fun at all the saccharine Disney fairy stories, with three blind mice; seven dwarfs; and mama, papa, and baby bears, et. al. A fitting Dreamwork's revenge. Angry, Shrek goes to see the King and strikes a deal to retrieve Princess Fiona, so he can get his swamp back to himself. Along the way, motor-mouth Donkey (Murphy) tags along, much to Shrek's aggravation. The pair go to the castle where Fiona awaits rescue, fight off a pink dragon with a hot crush on Donkey, and start walking back to the Kingdom of Far, Far Away to return Fiona to her parents and Lord Farquaar (Lithgow), who wants to marry her. Eventually, Shrek and Fiona develop a mutual attraction, but cannot fall in love until Fiona shares her secret. Of course, it takes a lot of convincing to get Fiona's parents, the King and Queen, to agree. What an entertaining way to tell the truth of true love – it's in the heart, not the outer physical appearance. Shrek 2 and 3 continue the saga about royal family complications.

DVD Release/Run Time	:	2001/108 minutes
Director	:	Andrew Adamson
Cast	:	Mike Myers, Eddie Murphy, Cameron Diaz, John Lithgow

Laugh & Cry Movie Rating System

Relationships	>	Lovers
Finding Love	>	30s
Overcoming Obstacles	>	Class Prejudice

Sideways

Sideways is a very funny buddy road trip, a slapstick comedy of 40-something men in midlife crisis, and a romantic ensemble of possible second chances. Jack (Church), a failed actor now scraping by as a voice talent, and Miles (Giamatti), a failed novelist, teacher, and alcoholic wine lover, take off for a frat-boy week of golf, wine drinking, and trouble one week before Jack's marriage. They set off to Solvang in the heart of California's premier pinot noir region. Through the side-splitting silliness and underlying sadness, a very moving love story emerges as Miles, nudged by Jack, finally approaches wine bar waitress Maya (Madsen), whom he has admired from afar for years at his favorite restaurant. He spends time with Maya and begins to see the possibility that his dreams may not be over after all. Maya's speech about wine and love will leave your palate thirsty and your heart melted. The uplifting ending will make you ready to watch the movie again. Won an Oscar for Best Adapted Screenplay and nominated for four others: Best Picture, Best Director, Best Supporting Actor, and Best Supporting Actress (Madsen).

DVD Release/Run Time	:	2005/126 minutes
Director	:	Alexander Payne
Cast	:	Paul Giamatti, Thomas Haden Church, Virginia Madsen, Sandra Oh

Laugh & Cry Movie Rating System

Relationships	>	Friends, Lovers
Finding Love	>	40s
Transitions	>	Marrying

Sleepless in Seattle

Get out the tissues for this great laugh-and-cry screwball, "love at first voice" comedy, which pays tribute to the contrived tearjerkers of the past. A Baltimore newspaper reporter Annie Reed (Ryan), engaged to her boring, allergic dweeb publisher Walter (Pullman), hears a young son Jonah Baldwin (Malinger) on a call-in radio show pleading for a new wife for his widowed Seattle architect father Sam (Hanks). Annie falls for the father when she hears his sad, tear-choked voice. Complete with goofy shots of the U.S. map with airplane routes from Seattle to Baltimore, the rest of the film is spent creating ingenious ways to unite this bi-coastal couple. Annie talks her editor Becky (O'Donnell) into a business trip to Seattle to research the story, but chickens out on actually meeting Sam there. True to its predecessors, the finale takes place at the top of the Empire State Building on Valentine's Day. For more tissue soakers, check out this sudsy story of illicit romance and separation in three previous forms, the classic starring Cary Grant/Deborah Kerr in the 1957 *An Affair to Remember*; comedic Irene Dunne/Charles Boyer in the superb 1939 *Love Affair*; and Warren Beatty/Annette Benning in the tired 1994 remake, also called *Love Affair*.

DVD Release/Run Time	:	1993/104 minutes
Director	:	Norah Ephron
Cast	:	Tom Hanks, Meg Ryan, Rosie O'Donnell, Rita Wilson,
		Victor Garber, Ross Malinger, Bill Pullman

Laugh & Cry Movie Rating System

Relationships	>	Lovers
Finding Love	>	30s
Transitions	>	Courting, Losing Mate
Overcoming Obstacles	>	Loss

Some Like It Hot

Comedy doesn't get any better than this fresh, fast paced cross-dressing, mistaken identity tale of two musicians on the lam from the Chicago mob after they inadvertently witness the St. Valentine's Day massacre. The only gig that can pay their way out of town is an all-girl band headed on a sleeper train for Miami. Sax player Joe/Josephine (Curtis) and bass player Jerry/ Daphne have to keep reminding themselves that they're supposed to be girls in the train berths with the band. When Joe falls for singer Sugar Kane Kowalczyk (Monroe), he poses as a millionaire Junior and invites her on Osgood Fielding III's yacht (Brown), while Daphne has to keep Osgood dancing all night. When the mobsters show up for a convention in Miami, Joe and Jerry realize their disguise has to keep them out of danger. Spectacular performances by Lemmon, Curtis, and Monroe create a perennial delight. This raucous film makes every list of best movies and comedies – AFI, Premiere, Entertainment Weekly, etc. – for very good reason. It's HOT!

DVD Release/Run Time	:	1959/119 minutes
Director	:	Billy Wilder
Cast	:	Jack Lemmon, Tony Curtis, Marilyn Monroe, Joe E. Brown

Laugh & Cry Movie Rating System

Work & Prosperity	>	Collaborate with Colleagues
Relationships	>	Lovers, Colleagues & Co-workers
Finding Love	>	30s
Transitions	>	Courting
Overcoming Obstacles	>	Sexual Prejudice, Entrapment

Something New

Here's a truly funny twist on the girl-meets-boy tale. An L.A. cotillion buppie (Lathan), on her accounting firm's partner fast track, can't believe she's falling for her cute, blond, blue-eyed landscape architect (Baker). He certainly doesn't fit any of her long list of must-have qualities in a man. And then an Ideal Black Man (Underwood) shows up to make her choices even more perplexing. Well-acted and scripted, it's a rare story that actually shows a couple falling in love, scene by amusing scene. The pedicure scene where the architect first introduces color into her beige corporate life is as sexy as PG-13 can get. A hip soundtrack underscores the fun and keeps drop-kicking the humorous action along.

DVD Release/Run Time	:	2006/100 minutes
Director	:	Sanaa Hamri
Cast	:	Sanaa Lathan, Simon Baker, Blair Underwood, Alfre Woodard

Laugh & Cry Movie Rating System

Work & Prosperity	>	Realizing Dreams
Relationships	>	Lovers
Finding Love	>	30s
Transitions	>	Achieving Career Goals, Courting
Overcoming Obstacles	>	Racial Prejudice, Class Prejudice

Something to Talk About

There's no better observer of American culture than an outsider. In this case, Swedish director Lasse Hallstrom (*What's Eating Gilbert Grape?, The Hoax, Chocolat*), with a sharp screenplay by Callie Khouri (*Thelma & Louise*), examines the King family dynamics – parents Wyly (Duvall) and Grace (Rowlands), still bickering about affairs past, frustrated daughter Grace (Roberts), who manages the family horse breeding business, and spot-on wise-cracking daughter Emma Ray (Sedgewick). The movie opens with Grace in an emotional meltdown, so distracted she frequently drives away forgetting her nine year-old daughter Caroline. Married to her college sweetheart Eddie Bichon (Quaid) for 10 years, Grace finally cracks when she discovers he's been having an affair. She moves back in with her parents. We don't often see honest portrayals of upper class American families, but this witty telling is amusing, entertaining, and wise. The outstanding cast delivers believable characters you actually care about. Sedgwick received a Golden Globe nomination for her hilarious depiction of the cynical sister who's seen it all. A great score punches up the comic moments, with Bonnie Raitt singing the title song.

DVD Release/Run Time	:	1995/106 minutes
Director	:	Lasse Hallstrom
Cast	:	Julia Roberts, Dennis Quaid, Kyra Sedgewick, Robert Duvall, Gena Rowlands

Laugh & Cry Movie Rating System

Work & Prosperity	>	Balancing Work & Family
Relationships	>	Married Couples, Multi-Generational Family
Finding Love	>	30s
Transitions	>	Achieving Career Goals
Overcoming Obstacles	>	Entrapment

Starting Over

This is a humorous look at midlife divorced Phil Potter's (Reynolds) confusion over falling in love again with insecure teacher Marilyn Holmberg (Clayburgh), before he's completely severed emotional ties to his neurotic ex-wife, singer Jessica (Bergen). When Jessica shows up to make another play for Phil and rekindle their romance with a song she's written him, Phil knows he has to make a choice once and for all. A fresh, witty script provides an upbeat take on the heart's twists and wrenching turns during and after a divorce as Phil navigates the murky road of letting go of his married relationship that never really worked, and moving into a new commitment free of his old emotional baggage. Bergen's performance singing Jessica's song is absolutely hilarious.

DVD Release/Run Time	:	1979/106 minutes
Director	:	Alan J. Pakula
Cast	:	Burt Reynolds, Jill Clayburgh, Candice Bergen

Laugh & Cry Movie Rating System

Relationships	>	Lovers, Divorced Couples
Finding Love	>	30s
Transitions	>	Courting, Divorcing
Overcoming Obstacles	>	Loss

Strictly Ballroom

This is an over-the-top, Down Under parody of Australian ballroom dancing competition by Baz Luhrmann (*Moulin Rouge!*). Ballroom dancing teachers Shirley (Thompson) and Doug Hastings (Otto) are at odds with their very talented son Scott (Mecurio). They've groomed him since age six to win the Pan-Pacific Championship. But headstrong Scott loves to dance in his own way and flouts the strict rules, discouraging winning partners, shocking the judges, and throwing his mother into an absolute tizzy. After losing several qualified partners, Scott ends up dancing with Fran (Morice), a rather awkward, unattractive beginner, whose flamenco dancer father teaches Scott the traditional steps. This tongue-in-cheek spoof shows the hilarious exasperation of parents who project their own unfulfilled dreams on their rebellious offspring. The finale, where Scott enters the dance floor on his knees dressed in toreador suit, is breathtaking and, just guessing here, probably not in the dance competition rule book.

DVD Release/Run Time	:	1992/94 minutes
Director	:	Baz Luhrmann
Cast	:	Paul Mercurio, Tara Morice, Bill Hunter, Pat Thompson, Barry Otto

Laugh & Cry Movie Rating System

Work & Prosperity	>	Realizing Dreams, Loving Your Work
Relationships	>	Lovers, Parent/Child
Finding Love	>	20s
Transitions	>	Courting, Achieving Career Goal
Overcoming Obstacles	>	Creative Expression, Entrapment

The Sure Thing

If you're tired of the teen romantic gross-out trend, from *American Pie* to *Superbad*, then this endearing, character-driven film is the perfect anecdote for you. It's an engaging story about how two students in an Eastern college really fall in love – shyly and slowly. Walt Gibson (Cusack) develops a crush on Alison Bradbury (Zuniga) in his English class, but she rejects him. At Christmas, the couple is thrown together in a cross-country trip home to L.A., which is a good excuse to fight, make up, share experiences, and start falling in love. Walt has been promised a date with a "sure thing" by his California hometown buddy. Alison is meeting her boyfriend in L.A. They both begin to see their commitments in a new light, when she visits her boring fiancé, and he half-heartedly checks out "the sure thing" his buddy has promised him. Even though you know where this story is going from the beginning, one thing is for sure, you'll enjoy the journey, maybe more than once.

DVD Release/Run Time	:	1985/94 minutes
Director	:	Rob Reiner
Cast	:	John Cusack, Daphne Zuniga, Anthony Edwards, Boyd Gaines, Tim Robbins

Laugh & Cry Movie Rating System

Relationships	>	Lovers
Finding Love	>	College Years
Transitions	>	Courting
Overcoming Obstacles	>	Entrapment

Sweet Home Alabama

This is a sweet Southern riff on the possibility of everlasting childhood love, even when you're all grown up. The pre-pubescent attraction between Melanie (Witherspoon) and Jake (Lucas) begins on a stormy beach hunting down buried glass made from sand that has been struck by lightning, and ends with a bitter teenage shotgun wedding and miscarriage. Ten years later, Melanie is an up-and-coming New York fashion designer engaged to the son (Dempsey) of the New York City mayor (Bergen). She is forced to return to her small Alabama home town to finalize the divorce from Jake, who's been resisting all these years. Things get complicated when Jake doesn't cooperate and the mayor starts snooping into Melanie's past. Turns out, Melanie has reinvented herself for the fashion press that hides some trailer trash secrets. But Jake hasn't been upfront about what he's been up to either. There are lots of hilarious confrontations between the Alabama hicks and the big city sophisticates, including Melanie's Civil War re-enactor daddy (Ward) and jam-making mama (Place) and the Southern plantation wedding. Who says lightning can't strike twice in the same place?

DVD Release/Run Time	:	2002/108 minutes
Director	:	Andy Tennant
Cast	:	Reese Witherspoon, Josh Lucas, Patrick Dempsey, Candice Bergen, Mary Kay Place, Fred Ward

Laugh & Cry Movie Rating System

Relationships	>	Lovers
Finding Love	>	30s
Transitions	>	Divorcing

The Tao of Steve

A most unlikely babe magnet, Dex (Logue) is a paunchy, part-time kindergarten bus driver slacker and a philosopher of the way Zen Buddhism, the Tao, and Steve McQueen movies can be combined to make him irresistible to women. He's figured out the three essential rules and he can't keep the ladies away, to the amazement of his underachieving friends. But things change when Dex goes to his 10-year college reunion and reconnects with his college sweetheart, who is coming to Santa Fe to design sets for the Opera Festival. This clever 1990 Sundance favorite, with Jury Awards to actor Donal Logue and director Jennifr (that's not a typo) Goodman, is a thinking person's romantic tale with an endearing visual casting twist that you don't normally see when the sexual roles are reversed. Well, maybe in a John Water's movie like *Hairspray*. This quirky film provides interesting insight into the phenomena of why women are more forgiving than men in the physical looks department. Set in stunning, rarely filmed Santa Fe, this fresh, funny take on the boy-meets-girl story will leave you feeling happy, warmhearted, and perhaps just a bit wiser.

DVD Release/Run Time	:	1990/90 minutes
Director	:	Jenniphr Goodman
Cast	:	Donal Logue, Greer Goodman, Ayelet Kaznelson

Laugh & Cry Movie Rating System

Relationships	>	Lovers
Finding Love	>	30s
Transitions	>	Courting

Terms of Endearment

This story of the bittersweet relationship of a domineering, perfectionist mother Aurora (MacLaine) and her joyful, happy-go-lucky daughter Emma (Winger) expresses the real-life blend of the highs of comic pleasures and the lows of sadness and hurts. Aurora, a frustrated Houston widow, hasn't had a date since her husband died years before, although she has a group of gentlemen who chastely hang around for her dinner parties. When she takes the uncomfortable plunge back into courting, Aurora makes an unlikely choice for a control freak – her next door neighbor Garrett Breedlove (Nicholson), a swinging bachelor astronaut. Emma marries a professor, Flap Horton (Daniels), who has a wandering eye for coeds. They have three children. Aurora does not approve. Then something unpredictable happens to shift the tone of this tale from an upbeat comedy to a three-handkerchief ending. Just like life. James L. Brooks won three Oscars for Best Director, Best Picture and Best Screenplay based on Larry McMurtry's novel. MacLaine and Nicholson also received Best Acting Oscars.

DVD Release/Run Time	:	1983/129 minutes
Director	:	James L. Brooks
Cast	:	Debra Winger, Shirley MacLaine, Jack Nicholson, Jeff Daniels, Danny DeVito

Laugh & Cry Movie Rating System

Relationships	>	Lovers, Parent/Child
Finding Love	>	College Years, 30s, 50s
Transitions	>	Courting, Marrying, Losing Mate
Overcoming Obstacles	>	Entrapment, Loss

There's Something About Mary

Crude, rude, and riotous from start to finish, in an over-the-top high school dude way, *There's Something About Mary* raised the 90s comedy bar to new heights. Yet underneath sidesplitting sight gags, there is a sweet love story of terminal geek Ted (Stiller), who scores a senior prom date with blonde bombshell Mary (Diaz) because he is kind to her autistic brother. Unfortunately, Ted is unable to attend the dance due to a very funny bathroom run-in with a zipper. Fast forward thirteen years, Ted is still thinking about Mary and decides to hire prevaricating private detective Pat Healy (Dillon) to find her. When Pat tracks her down in Miami, he decides to keep the comely Mary for himself. The comical war dance for Mary's heart begins with one uproarious fracas after another, but ending on a surprisingly loveable note.

DVD Release/Run Time	:	1998/119 minutes
Director	:	Bobby Farrelly & Peter Farrelly
Cast	:	Cameron Diaz, Matt Dillon, Ben Stiller

Laugh & Cry Movie Rating System

Relationships	>	Lovers
Finding Love	>	Teens, 30s
Transitions	>	Courting
Overcoming Obstacles	>	Mental Abilities

The Thomas Crown Affair

This stylish 90s comedy-thriller update of the McQueen-Dunaway classic has Thomas Crown (Brosnan) as a bored billionaire financial geek heisting art from the Metropolitan Art Museum, where he's presumably above suspicion since he's a large contributor and board member. The lively score teases the tension to the beat of Nina Simone's *Sinnerman* and sets the tone for this delightful cat and mouse caper romance. Catherine Banning (Russo), a gorgeous London-based insurance detective, intrigues commitment-phobe Crown because she is on to his clever game. Jaded NY Police detective McCann (Leary) doesn't have time for spoiled rich people. Russo's performance proves women over 40 can be beautiful, sexy, and smart and still have a shot at getting her man. It's a fun adventure fantasy about the life styles of the rich and famous, with stunning art, fabulous homes, fancy balls, and private jet trips to Caribbean islands. What more could a person want, at least for 90 minutes?

DVD Release/Run Time	:	1999/98 minutes
Director	:	John McTiernan
Cast	:	Pierce Brosnan, Rene Russo, Denis Leary, Faye Dunaway

Laugh & Cry Movie Rating System

Work & Prosperity	>	Realizing Dreams
Relationships	>	Lovers
Finding Love	>	40s
Transitions	>	Courting

The Truth About Cats & Dogs

This clever feminist brains-versus-beauty update on the Cyrano de Bergerac story examines British photographer Brian's (Chaplin) on-air attraction to a witty talk-radio veterinarian Abby (Garofalo), who doubts her cute five-foot tall, brunette physical allure. Brian calls Abby for advice about his dog Hank. When Brian asks to meet her in person, Abby arranges for him to meet her dimwitted, but physically stunning six-foot neighbor Noelle (Thurman) instead. Abby continues to talk with Brian on the phone. One of their late-night conversations, involving a tuna sandwich raised to sexy new heights, brings Brian to her apartment building expecting more. Abby chickens out when he gets there and speaks to him from her balcony with ridiculous excuses of why they can't meet. As the ruse spins out of control, Brian professes his love to Noelle/Abby, who doesn't know how to react. Meanwhile, the real Abby can't figure out how to come clean with Brian, convinced he's only interested in Noelle's beauty. When Brian does figure it out, he is furious with Abby. It takes Hank the dog and a pair of roller skates to finally bring them together.

DVD Release/Run Time	:	1996/97 minutes
Director	:	Michael Lehmann
Cast	:	Janeane Garofalo, Uma Thurman, Ben Chaplin

Laugh & Cry Movie Rating System

Relationships	>	Lovers, Friends
FindingLove	>	30s
Transitions	>	Courting
Overcoming Obstacles	>	Entrapment. Self-Esteem

Tune in Tomorrow

This perfectly delightful slapstick romance is about a young writer, Martin Loader (Reeves), and his aunt-by-marriage Aunt Julia (Hershey). After years apart, they reconnect in 1950s New Orleans and marry, even though Julia is 15 years his senior. The couple joins a radio soap opera show run by a wacky impresario Pedro Carmichael (Falk). When Pedro discovers the truth about Martin and Aunt Julia's relationship, he starts stirring up real-life conflict under the impish guise of romantic counsel. He does not want to run out of ideas to keep feeding his soap opera story mill. When the couple realizes they are being used, even more kooky chaos ensues. This story is based on Peruvian novelist Mario Vargas Llosa's own experience, and his novel *Aunt Julia and the Scriptwriter*. Wynton Marsalis's score adds authentic 50s New Orleans jazz flavor to punctuate the amorous comic mayhem. Don't miss this loving little treasure!

DVD Release/Run Time	:	1990/90 minutes
Director	:	Jon Ameil
Cast	:	Barbara Hershey, Keanu Reeves, Peter Falk

Laugh & Cry Movie Rating System

Work & Prosperity	>	Loving Your Work, Collaborate with Colleagues
Relationships	>	Boss/Employee, Married Couples
Finding Love	>	Radical Age Difference
Transitions	>	Marrying, Achieving Career Goals
Overcoming Obstacles	>	Creative Expression

Twelfth Night

Veteran Shakespearean writer/director Trevor Nunn updates the Bard's comic tale of gender confusion, cross-dressing, and the pursuit of love into the Victorian era. Look-alike brother Sebastian (MackIntosh) and sister Viola (Stubbs) are shipwrecked and believe the other has perished in the accident. Viola, to protect herself, dresses in her brother's military clothes and calls herself Cesario. Count Orsino (Stephens), in love with Olivia (Bonham-Carter) who spurns his advances, sends Cesario to plead his case for him. The plan backfires when Olivia falls for Cesario. Then Orsino starts to have disturbing feelings for the disguised Cesario. Lots of raucous complications are thrown into the mix, as Feste (Kingsley), the fool, narrates the amusing action for the audience. In Shakespeare's time, this plot was even sillier because men played all roles. The part Viola would have been played by a man, acting as a woman, who disguises herself as a man. Are you still with me? It makes *Tootsie, Priscilla, Queen of the Desert,* and *To Woo Fong* gender bending sound positively simple.

DVD Release/Run Time	:	1996/134 minutes
Director	:	Trevor Nunn
Cast	:	Imogen Stubbs, Steven Mackintosh, Helena Bonham Carter, Ben Kingsley, Imelda Staunton, Toby Stephens

Laugh & Cry Movie Rating System

Relationships	>	Lovers, Siblings
Finding Love	>	20s
Overcoming Obstacles	>	Sexual Prejudice

Two for the Road

Here's a rare and extraordinarily honest look at the marriage of a man, Mark Wallace (Finney), and a woman, Joanna (Hepburn), who grow as individuals and as a couple over a 12-year period, from college into their early 30s. The film presents the Wallace's story in short snippets of flash forwards and flash backs. It starts with Mark and Joanna as idealistic English college kids hitchhiking through the French countryside, and ends with them in the French Riviera with Mark, a work-obsessed successful architect with no personal life, and Joanna feeling neglected and about to start another affair. Writer Fredric Raphael wanted to create a film in which the characters "live their lives." A perennial emotional favorite, each movie lover's response to this tale is uniquely their own, based on their experience and ability to identify with Mark, Joanna, and/or their relationship over time. You come to realize how demonstrating their love and affection at the start can end up calling each other bitch and bastard in mutual bitterness. This film is a wonderful gauge of the evolution of your own understanding of male/female relationships.

DVD Release/Run Time	:	1967/112 minutes
Director	:	Stanley Donen
Cast	:	Audrey Hepburn, Albert Finney, Eleanor Bron, William Daniels

Laugh & Cry Movie Rating System

Work & Prosperity	>	Balancing Work & Family
Relationships	>	Husband/Wife
Finding Love	>	College, 20s, 30s
Transitions	>	Courting, Marrying
Overcoming Obstacles	>	Entrapment

Waitress

This clever comic vision tells a Southern tale about talented pie-baking waitress Jenna (Russell), trapped in an abusive marriage to Earl (Sisto), who dreams of escape by winning a baking contest. Her hopes are dashed when she learns she's pregnant. As Jenna creates a new pie recipe every day, she channels her conflicted feelings into pie names like "Pregnant, Miserable Loser Pie, Flambe, Of Course". She falls into a hilarious, heated affair with her married Ob/Gyn, Dr. Jim Pomatter (Fillion), who has a waitress fantasy. Then Jenna bakes up "I Can't Have No Affair Because It's Wrong and Earl Will Kill Me Pie, Hold the Banana". Andy Griffiths brilliantly bookends his Mayberry years in a delectable performance as Joe, the diner owner, who has a crush on more than just Jenna's pies. Here's a movie that takes you on a delicious roller coaster ride through comical and poignant moments without being sappy or cheesy, and leaves you feeling happy, uplifted, and ready for a piece of pie a la mode.

DVD Release/Run Time	:	2007/108 minutes
Director	:	Adrienne Shelley
Cast	:	Keri Russell, Cheryl Hines, Andy Griffiths, Jeremy Sisto, Nathan Fillion

Laugh & Cry Movie Rating System

Work & Prosperity	>	Realizing Dreams
Relationships	>	Married Couples
Finding Love	>	30s
Transitions	>	Achieving Career Goals
Overcoming Obstacles	>	Entrapment

Walking and Talking

This mid-90s indie film tells about the up and down relationship of two thirty something women, Amelia (Keener) and Laura (Heche), who were friends as girls and are now roommates in Manhattan. Laura is a therapist and has just become engaged to Frank (Field), although she has her doubts. Adrift, Amelia moves out. She has recently broken up with her boyfriend Andrew (Schreiber), although they're still friends, and surprises herself by falling for a not-so-attractive geeky video store clerk Bill (Corrigan). Life in the big city for Amelia and Laura covers the whole gamut of couple challenges including getting engaged, doubts about commitment, getting married, breaking up and staying friends, bad dates with geeks, long-distance phone sex, routine sex after engagement, and jealousy. Through it all, the women try to figure out how to remain true to themselves, stay friends, and find fulfillment with their men. The superb cast enhances this amusing and sympathetic look at the bonds that hold women and men together, and pull them apart.

DVD Release/Run Time	:	1996/86 minutes
Director	:	Nicole Holofcener
Cast	:	Catherine Keener, Anne Heche, Todd Field,
		Liev Schreiber, Kevin Corrigan

Laugh & Cry Movie Rating System

Relationships	>	Lovers, Friends
Finding Love	>	30s
Transitions	>	Courting, Marrying
Overcoming Obstacles	>	Entrapment

The Wedding Planner

Wedding jitters and career ambitions comically collide when Type-A San Francisco wedding planner Mary Fiore (Lopez) unknowingly breaks her profession's biggest taboo – falling for the groom, Steve Edison (McConaughey). Mary is preparing for her biggest wedding event yet for young business tycoon Fran Donolly (Wilson) and her college sweetheart, whom she calls Eddie. Mary hopes the event will get her that big promotion, but her busy-ness is a way to cover up her humiliation of being jilted at her own rehearsal dinner. In the meantime, she has to fend off the amusing advances of her family's Italian friend, Massimo (Chambers). Before Mary learns the truth about Steve/Eddie, she starts making her own nuptial plans. But the path to happily-ever-after turns out not to be that straight forward. This San Francisco treat of a romance leaves you with a sweet feeling where you'd like to leave your heart.

DVD Release/Run Time	:	2001/103 minutes
Director	:	Adam Shankman
Cast	:	Jennifer Lopez, Matthew McConaughey, Bridgette Wilson, Justin Chambers

Laugh & Cry Movie Rating System

Relationships	>	Lovers
Finding Love	>	30s
Transitions	>	Marrying

When Harry Met Sally

This flawless feel-good romance about friendship and fear of commitment strikes the perfect tone to explore the question of whether a man and a woman can be friends, even after having sex. Upon college graduation, Sally Albright (Ryan) drives Harry Burns (Crystal) from Chicago to New York where Harry pontificates that men and women cannot be friends, to Sally's disgust. Fast forward five years, they meet again on a plane trip. Sally is dating and Harry is about to get married, and they still can't stand each other. A bickering, platonic friendship starts up again when they meet another five years later. Harry is devastated by his divorce and Sally just broke up with her boyfriend. They start hanging out as friends and dating others, but one night Sally asks Harry to come over late because she just learned that her ex-boyfriend is getting married. Sally is distraught, and, as Harry comforts her, they end up having sex – to Harry's horror. Inspired improvisations by Crystal and Ryan enliven a terrific Nora Ephron script, including the classic Ryan faked orgasm scene. The close out of real-life older married couples recalling how they met leaves you feeling bouyant with proof positive that you can be friends, have sex, and stay married.

DVD Release/Run Time	:	1986/96 minutes
Director	:	Rob Reiner
Cast	:	Billy Crystal, Meg Ryan, Carrie Fisher, Bruno Kirby

Laugh & Cry Movie Rating System

Relationships	>	Lovers, Friends
Finding Love	>	College Years, 30s
Transitions	>	Courting
Overcoming Obstacles	>	Entrapment

While You Were Sleeping

This sweet fable shows what happens when your fantasies come true, but don't always turn out like you'd plan. Lucy (Bullock) is a lonely yet endearing Chicago El train token taker with no family left. She dreams of a trip to Florence, Italy and a relationship with a handsome lawyer Peter Callahan (Gallagher) who passes through her booth every morning. One day he's pushed under the El and Lucy rescues him. At the hospital, she is mistaken for his fiancé. The mixup spirals out of control when his large family shows up at the hospital and Peter's coma continues for days. Too shy to speak the truth, Lucy is included in their Christmas gatherings. She begins to fall for his brother Jack (Pullman), a furniture designer, who reluctantly runs the family's antiques business. It's a fun romp that showcases Sandra Bullock's comedic skills and leaves you feeling warmhearted, hopeful, and cheered that we're not alone after all.

DVD Release/Run Time	:	1995/103 minutes
Director	:	Jon Turteltaub
Cast	:	Sandra Bullock, Bill Pullman, Peter Gallagher

Laugh & Cry Movie Rating System

Relationships	>	Lovers
Finding Love	>	30s
Transitions	>	Courting

You've Got Mail

This is director Nora Ephron's Electronic Age update and mash up of two classic 40s romantic comedies – *The Shop Around the Corner* and *In the Good Old Summertime*, with a dash of *Pride and Prejudice* – set in the tony Upper West Side of New York. Children's bookstore owner Kathleen Kelly (Ryan) is being forced out of business by big chain Fox Books, building a new store a few blocks away. Restless in her relationship with an arrogant, neglectful columnist (Kinnear), she starts up an anonymous email correspondence with Joe Fox (Hanks), heir to the book chain, and starts pouring out her deepest thoughts and frustrations to him. Joe is intrigued with the correspondence, despite being in a disaffected relationship with a Type A book editor (Posey) "who would make coffee nervous." The rest of the movie has fun showing how Joe discovers Kathleen's true identity, but doesn't fess up that he's her email pal. As Joe realizes he's fallen in love with Kathleen, he has to figure out how to overcome his pride and woo Kathleen, despite her prickly prejudice. The DVD extras are wonderful, especially the Upper West Side map and narration of the real places there that serve as another character in the movie.

DVD Release / Run Time	:	1998 / 119 minutes
Director	:	Nora Ephron
Cast	:	Tom Hanks, Meg Ryan, Dave Chappelle, Parker Posey, Greg Kinnear

Laugh & Cry Movie Rating System

Work & Prosperity	:	Realizing Dreams, De-structuring Workplace
Relationships	:	Lovers
Finding Love	:	30s
Transitions	:	Losing Job, Courting
Overcoming Obstacles	:	Class Prejudice

APPENDIX

A

Movie Club Tips and Tricks

Define Your Movie Club's Purpose

The first issue to address is what your movie club's focus will be. You must decide what type of experience you and your fellow movie lovers want to engage in before, during, and after viewing the movie. Next, you must narrow your focus to certain types of film, at least initially. For example, you could explore certain types of film or topics, such as:

- Movies that entertain and uplift
- Intellectual movies and documentaries that can be analyzed for political, social, or psycho drama
- Movies for personal growth

Movie Club Logistics

The next challenge to address is figuring out the who, what, where, when, and how of the movie club. The type of people you invite into the group frames the ambience of the meetings. The different kinds of movies you view shape the discussions. Where you meet and how often influences the experience as well.

- **Who** you select for your movie club determines the tenor of the club meetings. You must decide what type of potential members you want to include: women, men, or couples. The people included

in the movie club will shape the future topics of the meeting. The ideal size for group discussion is around 6-8 people, but you will want to include 10-12 people because not every person can attend every meeting.

- **What** type of films does the club want to view — new releases vs. DVDs and downloads? That will determine where you actually see the films.
- **Where** do you want to see the movies? Meeting as a group, there are four possibilities:
  1. New releases can only be seen in theaters. Sometimes it is difficult to plan in advance to see new movies because release dates change or films are only in theaters for a few weeks. Less than one month release timings are difficult to schedule for clubs that meet monthly.
  2. Movie groups can also attend revival movie theater showings together. Those theaters usually announce their film schedules at least three months in advance.
  3. DVDs and downloads can be shown in members' homes or in local meeting places, like community centers, churches, etc.
  4. View the film before you meet with the movie club members for the discussion.

- **When** to meet and how frequently you want the club to meet must also be decided. You have to figure out what time of day is most convenient for the group to meet and what day of the week. Monthly frequency usually work best for most social movie groups.
- **How** to eat or not to eat, depends on when you meet and where you are meeting.
  1. For meetings in theaters, decide whether the club members want to meet before or after the movie showing for snacks or meals. Lighter fare usually works best before the viewing.
  2. For meetings in members' homes, decide whether the food will be snacks or meals, what food the host will provide — drink only or food and drink, or if the group will bring potluck food and their own beverages.

Movie Club Roles and Responsibilities

Organizer: This person initiates the movie club, has a passion for film, and recruits compatible members to join the club.

Publicist: This person is responsible for communicating the What, Where, When of the next month's meeting via email, with a follow up email one week before the next meeting. The publicist might also scribe the meetings and email the meeting's highlights to members.

Distributor: For viewings, this person is responsible for making sure that everyone in the group has access to the DVD or streaming before the meeting through Netflix, Amazon, on demand, or the public library.

Discussion Leader: This person moderates the discussion to ensure there is enough time for each person to express their reactions to the film being discussed. The discussion leader facilitates the group's conversation and sees that no one person dominates the dialogue. There is no greater conversation stopper than to have one or more members of the group fall into the *In Living Color* Men on Film routine of "Loved It!" or "Hated It" with no further explanation of their visceral reaction. Worse yet, the discussion devolves into a bad View show with everyone talking at once, trying to shout down those who don't agree with them.

Backgrounder: This person presents information about the film, like "Making of .." documentary back story, bloopers, continuity gaffes, and/or cast biographical information.

Setting the Meeting Schedule

- Set the film schedule 3-6 months in advance, allowing for holiday and vacation hiatuses. Here are some examples for topics:
  1. New Releases
  2. One from each of AFI's Top 10 Genres: Animated, Fantasy, Gangster, Sci-Fi, Western, Sports, Mystery, Romantic Comedy, Courtroom Drama, and Epic
  3. Classic Films
  4. Page to Screen: Book + Movie – Which Is Better?

5. Documentary: Issues or Funny
6. Seasonal Movies

Fun Ways to Stimulate After-Movie Discussions

Here are conversation starters to enliven the conversation after viewing a movie with friends. Allow everyone to contribute. Keep focused on sharing the emotions that the movie generated for each person. You can't argue with a person's feelings, taste and emotional responses. If they laugh or cried and you didn't, both of you are right.

Allow ample time for each person to share their sentiments. Remember, great storytelling is about igniting the imagination, generating heart tugs and goose bumps, and inspiring a new point of view in the end. Everyone's emotional experience is different. So honor diverse reactions to the film among your group. Celebrate your differences. That's the fun of entertainment!

Here are 10 questions to stimulate a lively conversation after viewing a movie:

1. What was the theme of the film, and was that message effectively delivered?

2. Were there any questionable story elements or plot developments that distracted you from the theme?

3. How did you feel about that message? How were you expecting to feel after the movie? How did the movie actually affect you emotionally?

4. Did your mood change after watching the film? Did it change your perspective on the theme?

5. What had you heard about the film? Was it similar to your experience viewing the picture?

6. Would you want to see the film again? Why/why not?

7. Would you recommend or show this film to friends? How would you describe it to them?

8. If you'd seen the film before, did you feel the same way about it this

time? What changed? How have you changed? What motivated you to see the movie again?

9. Did you notice anything unique about the motion picture, like cinematography, costumes, etc., that enhanced your viewing experience?

10. What other movies or stories did this film remind you of? If you liked this movie, what other movies do you feel you might enjoy?

What ice-breaking questions do you use to invigorate your after-movie discussions with your friends?

B

Why Laughter Is the Best Medicine

A happy heart is good medicine.

Proverbs 17:22

Norman Cousins found that watching Marx Brothers movies gave him a few hours of pain relief as he was recovering from a life-threatening illness. He was so convinced about the therapeutic benefits of laughter that he funded my team's research effort in 1983 to scientifically validate the benefits of humor and laughing. And the discoveries are impressive.

We have documented that laughter activates the immune system. Our research results have proven that the physiological response produced by laughter is the opposite of what is seen in classical stress, supporting the conclusion that mirthful laughter is an eustress state – a state that produces healthy or positive emotions.

Our findings indicate that, after experiencing mirthful laughter, there is a general decrease in stress hormones and an increase in activity within the immune system, including:

- An increase in activated T cells (T lymphocytes). There are many T cells that await activation. Laughter appears to tell the immune system to "turn it up a notch".

- An increase in the antibody IgA (immunoglobulin A), which fights upper respiratory tract insults and infections.
- An increase in gamma interferon, which tells various components of the immune system to "turn on".
- An increase in Natural Killer Cell activity, cells that kill virally infected cells and tumor cells.

What is success? To laugh often and much.

Ralph Waldo Emerson, author

- An increase in IgG, the immunoglobulin produced in the greatest quantity in the body, as well as an increase in Complement 3, which helps antibodies to pierce dysfunctional or infected cells. The increase in both substances was only present while subjects watched a humorous video; moreover, subjects continued to show increased levels the next day, revealing a lingering effect. Laughter decreases "bad" stress. In our research, the study group exposed to mirthful humor decreased their "stress" hormones, which constrict blood vessels and suppress immune activity. For example, levels of epinephrine were lower in the group both during anticipation of humor and after exposure to humor.

Epinephrine levels remained down throughout the experiment. In addition, dopamine levels (as measured by dopac) were also decreased. Dopamine is involved in the "fight or flight response" and is associated with elevated blood pressure.

He who laughs, lasts.

Dr. Lee Berk, Loma Linda University

As a medical scientist, it is gratifying and fulfilling to continue to discover objective scientific data to support beliefs that many have held intuitively for centuries. This book serves as an innovative guide to finding movies that stimulate not only your sense of humor, but also your immune system. "He who laughs, lasts."

Dr. Lee Berk
Assistant Professor
Pathology, Laboratory Medicine, Preventive
Medicine, Health Promotion, and Education
Loma Linda University
Schools of Medicine and Public Health

C

Cathie Glenn Jennings Bio

Cathie Glenn Jennings was born and raised in a northern Ohio town of 2000 people which she experienced as a cross between *The Last Picture Show* and *Northern Exposure*. Her love of movies began in grade school at the Saturday matinee serials and TV reruns. In high school, her theatrical experiences closely mirrored *Waiting for Guffman*, right down to the gay drama director/chemistry teacher. As the oldest in a large musical family, Cathie navigated a complex childhood that was like an emotional mash up of *Unstrung Heroes*, *Corrina, Corrina*, and *Dan in Real Life*.

Cathie's closest Hollywood connection was her family looks. Her grandfather looked like he and John Wayne were separated at birth. Her mother resembled Mary Astor, down to Astor's hairstyle in The Maltese Falcon. Her father looked like E. G. Marshall in The Defenders. Unfortunately, Cathie looks more like the feminine version of E.G. than Mary Astor.

The day Neil Armstrong landed on the moon, Cathie moved to San Francisco. She ended up living on Montgomery Street, where the movies *The House on Telegraph Hill* and *Wild Parrots of Telegraph Hill* were shot. With a career focused on product launch and strategic marketing, her passion for movies led her to teaching seminars on how to use movies for team building and career coaching at corporations, colleges, and career centers.

Her love of romantic comedy has helped her laugh and cry her way through her own relationship roller coaster rides. After an unfortunate starter marriage to a lawyer and musician who resembled Mikhail Baryshnikov, Cathie learned to skip the wedded bliss bit. She became a serial monogamist with a track record of five to seven year relationships that included a Scandinavian-American marketing executive and sailor who looked like Spencer Tracy in his prime, a public relations executive and skier like Jack Lemmon in *Days of Wine and Roses* without the wine part, and a software sales executive who had a sad demise not as pretty as John Travolta in *Phenomena*. Like May West said, Cathie used to be Snow White, but she drifted.

Join conversations about romantic comedies and relationship dramas that entertain and enrich your life and fuel your dreams at
www.MovieGuideChickFlicks.com.

www.ingramcontent.com/pod-product-compliance
Lightning Source LLC
Chambersburg PA
CBHW052002090426
42741CB00008B/1519